✝ *We Sing and Praise* ✝

MUSIC SERIES FOR CATHOLIC SCHOOLS

We Sing and Blend

BY

SISTER CECILIA, S.C., M.F.A.

SUPERVISOR OF MUSIC, *Sisters of Charity of Seton Hill*
Greensburg, Pennsylvania

SISTER JOHN JOSEPH, C.S.J., Ph.D.

DIRECTOR OF DEPARTMENT OF MUSIC, *Fontbonne College*
St. Louis, Missouri

SISTER ROSE MARGARET, C.S.J., M.M.

SUPERVISOR OF MUSIC IN ELEMENTARY SCHOOLS
Sisters of Saint Joseph of Carondelet, St. Louis, Missouri

Illustrations by BERYL JONES, RUTH WOOD, BEATRICE DERWINSKI *and*
SISTER JOSEFA MARY, S.C.

Ginn and Company

Boston · New York · Chicago · Atlanta · Dallas · Palo Alto · Toronto

Acknowledgments

Acknowledgment is due to publishers, composers, and authors for permission to reprint songs and poems in this book, as follows:

The Apostleship of Prayer, "To the Trinity" (words only) by Paul Stauder, S.J., from the *Messenger of the Sacred Heart*; *Ave Maria*, "March Winds" (words only) by D.A.M.A.; The Boy Scouts Association, "We're All Together Again" from the *Boy Scout Songbook of England*; Bruce Publishing Company, "Hail, King of Kings!" (words only) from *A Lovely Gate Set Wide* by Sister Margaret Patrice, S.S.J.; *Children's Activities*, "When Spring Is Here" (words only) by Beth M. Jaeger; *The Commonweal*, "The Juniper Tree" (words only) by Eileen Duggan; Co-operative Recreation Service, Inc., "Sleep, My Baby" from *Work and Sing*, copyright 1948 by Cooperative Recreation Service, used by permission; Ginn and Company, "Wind Song" and "Work to Do" from the *New Educational Music Course*; "Donegal Fair," "Easter Bells" (melody only), "O Echo" (melody only), "Mother of Mine," "Old Black Crow," "The Raggle-Taggle Gypsies" (words only), "The River Man," all from the *Music Education Series*; Ginn and Company and the editors of *The World of Music*, "The Bamboo Screen," "The Bell Ringer," "Christmas Lullaby," "Deep in the Forest," "Down the Stream," "Early One Morning," "The Fisher Maiden," "The Fisherman of Gloucester," "Fisherman's Song," "Harvest Dance," "Harvest Hymn," "The Haymakers," "Ho! Every Sleeper, Waken!" "I'd Like to Be a Sailor" (melody only), "In the Lane," "The Little Donkey" (melody only), "Moon of Silver White" (words only), "My Bark Canoe," "My Donkey Diodoro," "My Home's in Montana," "Night in the Desert," "Our Land," "Pay with a Smile," "Pedro and Cita," "Pepita," "The Pipers of Balmoral," "Polish Dance" (melody only), "The Roving Cowboy," "The Santa Fe Trail," "Shepherd, Tell Us," "A Song of China," "Songs of Gold," "Sweet Betsy from Pike," "Wait for the Wagon," "When Poppies Close Their Eyes," "When the Chestnut Leaves Were Falling," "Winter Music" (words only); Ginn and Company and the editors of *Our Singing World*, "All around the Shu-Round," "The Brown Bird," "Deck the Hall," "Goin' to Leave Ol' Texas," "Good Night," "He Is Born, the Holy Child," "Hush-a-By, Baby," "Kookaburra," "Morning Song," "One More River," "Peacefully, My Baby, Sleep," "Shoo Fly," "The Sleighride," "Snow Is Falling," "Swing on the Corner"; Ginn and Company and the editors of *Faith and Freedom*, "Cattle Country" (words only) by Mary T. Synon, "I Heard a Bird Sing" (words only) by Oliver Herford; Ginn and Company, "The Campfire" (words only) by James S. Tippett from *Buckingham Bookshelf*, "Bob White" (words only) by George Cooper from *Children's Literature* by DePew; Rufina McCarthy Helmer, estate of Denis McCarthy, "St. Joseph's Vigil" (words only) by Denis McCarthy; *Mine Magazine*, Publications for Catholic Youth, "Spring Song" (words only); Polanie Club, "The Quail Song" from *Treasures of Polish Songs*.

The words of "St. Patrick's Day" are used by courtesy of Sister M. Laurent, C.S.J.

In the case of some poems for which acknowledgment is not given, we have earnestly endeavored to find the original source and to procure permission for their use, but without success.

The contents of this book have received the approval of the DIOCESAN MUSIC COMMISSION, Boston, Massachusetts.

DEDICATION

This book is dedicated
to the Holy Spirit,
who has filled the hearts of the faithful
and kindled in them the fire of divine love.

Contents

Christmastide and After

Lent and Passiontide

Eastertide

Pentecost

We Sing the Mass

We Sing and Blend

After Pentecost

Come, Holy Spirit, Creator blest,
And in our hearts take up Thy rest.
Come with Thy grace and heavenly aid
To fill the hearts which Thou hast made.

Praise to the Lord

NEANDER-WINKWORTH

TRADITIONAL

1. Praise to the Lord, the Al-might-y, the King of cre - a - tion!
2. Praise to the Lord! Oh, let all that is in me a - dore Him!

Oh, my soul, praise Him for He is thy health and sal - va - tion!
All that has life and breath, now come with prais-es be - fore Him!

All ye who hear, now to His al - tar draw near;
Let the A - men sound from His peo - ple a - gain;

Join - ing in glad ad - o - ra - tion.
Now as we wor-ship be - fore Him.

Thine are the heavens, and thine is the earth: the world and the fulness thereof thou hast founded.

Psalm 88

In Nomine Patris

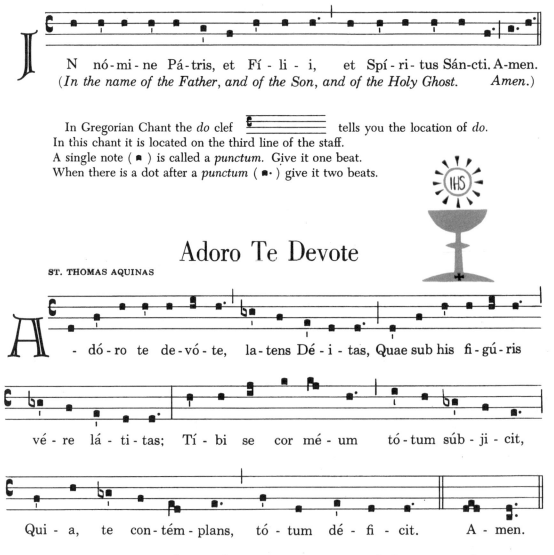

IN nó-mi-ne Pá-tris, et Fí-li-i, et Spí-ri-tus Sán-cti. A-men.
(*In the name of the Father, and of the Son, and of the Holy Ghost. Amen.*)

In Gregorian Chant the *do* clef ▆ tells you the location of *do*.
In this chant it is located on the third line of the staff.
A single note (▪) is called a *punctum*. Give it one beat.
When there is a dot after a *punctum* (▪·) give it two beats.

Adoro Te Devote

ST. THOMAS AQUINAS

A-dó-ro te de-vó-te, la-tens Dé-i-tas, Quae sub his fi-gú-ris

vé-re lá-ti-tas; Tí-bi se cor mé-um tó-tum súb-ji-cit,

Qui-a, te con-tém-plans, tó-tum dé-fi-cit. A-men.

A *neum* is a group of two or three notes sung on one vowel. Do you remember the names of these *neums*? Find them in the hymn.

    Podatus ▐   Sing the lower note first. Sing the upper note more softly.
    Clivis ▐   Sing the upper note first. Sing the second note more softly.
    Torculus ▲   There are three notes in a *torculus* group. The middle note is always the highest. Sing it more softly.

Adoro Te Devote

ST. THOMAS AQUINAS

A - dó - ro te de - vó - te, la - tens Dé - i - tas,
(I adore Thee devoutly, hidden God,)

Quae sub his fi - gú - ris vé - re lá - ti - tas:
(Who art truly hidden beneath these forms,)

Tí - bi se___ cor mé - um tó - tum súb - ji - cit,
(To Thee my heart submits itself entirely,)

Qui - a, te con - tém - plans, tó - tum dé - fi - cit. A - men.___
(Because in contemplating Thee, it finds itself wholly helpless.)

Compare this notation with the Gregorian notation.

Can you find the groups of notes on this page which would be *neums* in the Gregorian notation?

3

Salve Mater

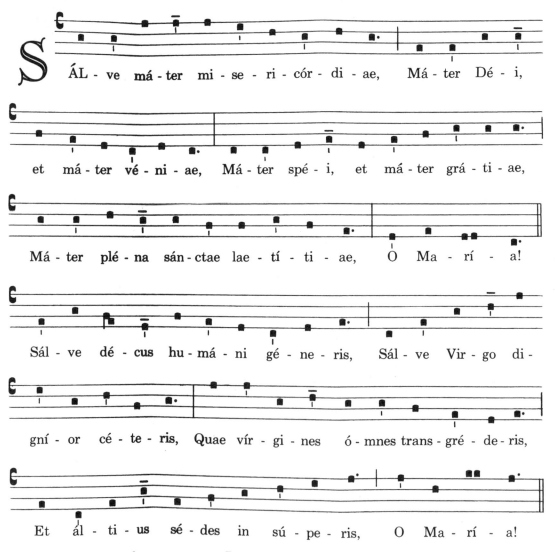

SÁL - ve má - ter mi - se - ri - cór - di - ae, Má - ter Dé - i,

et má - ter vé - ni - ae, Má - ter spé - i, et má - ter grá - ti - ae,

Má - ter plé - na sán - ctae lae - tí - ti - ae, O Ma - rí - a!

Sál - ve dé - cus hu - má - ni gé - ne - ris, Sál - ve Vir - go di -

gní - or cé - te - ris, Quae vír - gi - nes ó - mnes trans - gré - de - ris,

Et ál - ti - us sé - des in sú - pe - ris, O Ma - rí - a!

A short line over a note (◼) tells you to hold the note a little longer.
Ends of phrases are always sung softly in Gregorian Chant.

4

Praise the Lord, O my soul, in my life I will praise the Lord. I will sing to my God as long as I shall be.

Hymn of St. Francis

TRADITIONAL HYMN

1. Praise, oh praise our God and King, Hymns of ad - o - ra - tion sing.
2. Praise Him that He made the sun, Day by day His course to run,
3. Praise Him that He gave the rain To ma - ture the swell-ing grain,

For His mer - cies still en - dure, Ev - er_ faith - ful, ev - er sure.
And the sil - ver moon by night, Shin - ing with His gen - tle light.
And hath bid the fruit - ful field, Crops of_ pre - cious in-crease yield.

May the Lord Bless Thee

ST. FRANCIS of ASSISI   SISTER ALICE MARIE, O.S.U.

May the Lord bless thee and keep thee. May He show His face to thee and have

mer - cy. May He turn His coun-te-nance to thee, and give thee peace.

Notice that this melody is in free rhythm because it has no time signature.
Sing all the eighth notes evenly with a breath only after each quarter note.

Praise the Lord

so *la* *do*

1. O praise the Lord all you na - tions,
2. For all powerful to us is His mer - cy,
3. Glory be to the Father and to the Son,
4. As it was in the beginning, is now, and ever shall be,

praise Him all you peo - ples.
the Lord is true to His word for - ev - er.
and to the Ho - ly Spir - it.
world with out end. A - men.

Good Night

Translated by REV. VINCENT PISEK

CZECH FOLK SONG

mi

Good night, be - lov - ed, good night, good night; God keep you safe in His
Birds are a - sleep in the whis-p'ring tree, Soft blows the wind from the

watch-ful sight. Good night, dear, soft - ly sleep, Sweet be the dreams of your
mur-m'ring sea. Good night, dear, soft - ly sleep, Sweet be the dreams of your

slum - ber deep, Good night, dear, soft - ly sleep; Sweet be the dreams of your
slum - ber deep, Good night, dear, soft - ly sleep; Sweet be the dreams of your

slum - ber deep.
slum - ber deep. Good night, dear.

What other way could you write this time signature?

How many times do you find this rhythm pattern (♩ ♫♩ ♫|♩ ♩ ♩) repeated?

The Fisherman of Gloucester

ETHEL CROWNINSHIELD

TRADITIONAL

1. The Fish - er - man of Glouces-ter
2. The Fish - er - man of Glouces-ter

has weath-ered man - y gales.
has nei - ther hopes nor fears;

He's gaz - ing t'ward the o - pen sea and look-ing for the sails
He gaz - es t'ward the storm-y banks and out a - cross the years.

Of the fish - ing boats of Glouces-ter, from the port of miss-ing men;
For his heart is with the sail - ors in the port of miss-ing men;

1,2. The fish - ing boats of Glouces-ter that will nev - er come a - gain.

In a time signature the upper number tells how many beats there are in a measure. The lower number tells you the kind of note that gets one beat. Count the value of the notes and rests in various measures. They always equal two quarter notes.

Sailor's Hymn

TRANSLATED

FRENCH FOLK SONG

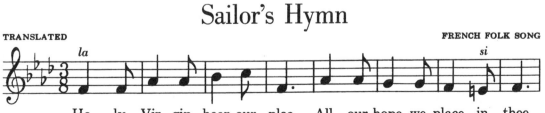

Ho - ly Vir - gin, hear our plea. All our hope we place in thee.
Vier - ge sainte ex - au - cez - nous, Notre es - poir est tout en vous!

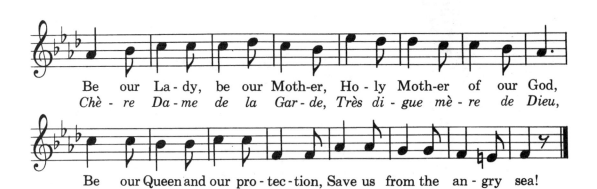

Be our La - dy, be our Moth-er, Ho - ly Moth-er of our God,
Chè - re Da - me de la Gar - de, Très di - gue mè - re de Dieu,

Be our Queen and our pro - tec - tion, Save us from the an - gry sea!
Soy - ez no - tre sau - ve - gar - de, Pour nous dé-fendre en tout lieu.

This hymn is often sung by French sailors.
Perhaps you can learn to sing it in French.

Fisherman's Song

BLANCHE JENNINGS THOMPSON   FINNISH FOLK SONG

1. Spread the nets out in the sun: Come, work, my lads, to - geth - er!
2. Ship the do - ries, hoist the sails! Oh, work, my lads, to - geth - er!

Mend the strands now, one by one. Oh, work, my lads, to - geth - er!
Out to meet the north-ern gales We'll sail, my lads, to - geth - er!

When the fleet puts out to sea, The nets must all be mend - ed.
Our good ship shall ride the storm, Though loud the winds be blow - ing.

When the fleet puts out to sea, The nets must all be mend - ed.
Our good ship shall ride the storm, Though loud the winds be blow - ing.

Do you remember how to sing the dotted quarter and eighth notes?

Pepita

Translated by
FRANCES FORD

SPANISH FOLK SONG

1. Sau - cy and dark is Pe - pi - ta,
2. Now see her spin - ning and whirl - ing,

Nev - er a rose could be sweet - er.
All her red rib - bons un - furl - ing!

When she comes click - ing her cas - ta - nets,
See how she flut - ters her cor - al fan,

Not a foot could be neat - er.
Gai - ly trip - ping and twirl - ing!

The time signature $\frac{6}{8}$ tells us there are two beats in a measure.
For each beat there will be one of the following rhythm patterns: (♪♪♪),
(♩.), or (♩ ♪).

I'm the Doctor Eisenbart[1]

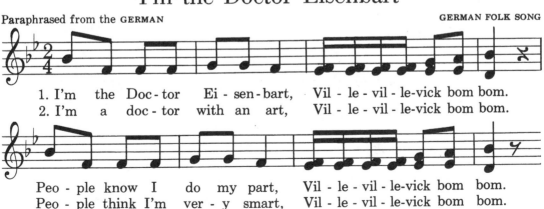

Paraphrased from the GERMAN

GERMAN FOLK SONG

1. I'm the Doc - tor Ei - sen - bart, Vil - le - vil - le - vick bom bom.
2. I'm a doc - tor with an art, Vil - le - vil - le - vick bom bom.

Peo - ple know I do my part, Vil - le - vil - le - vick bom bom.
Peo - ple think I'm ver - y smart, Vil - le - vil - le - vick bom bom.

[1]Pronounce *Eye-zen-bahrt.*

9

One More River

AMERICAN NEGRO

Not too fast

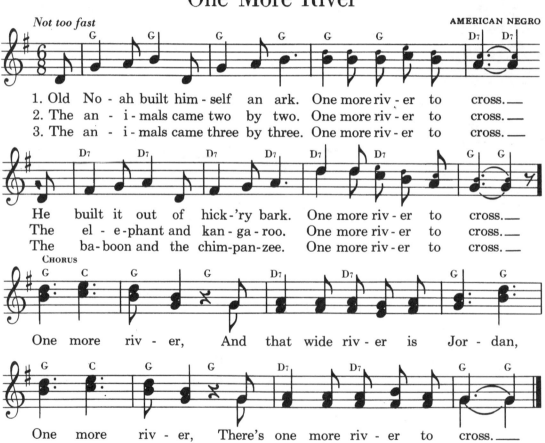

1. Old No - ah built him - self an ark. One more riv - er to cross.—
2. The an - i - mals came two by two. One more riv - er to cross.—
3. The an - i - mals came three by three. One more riv - er to cross.—

He built it out of hick -'ry bark. One more riv - er to cross.—
The el - e - phant and kan - ga - roo. One more riv - er to cross.—
The ba - boon and the chim - pan - zee. One more riv - er to cross.—

CHORUS

One more riv - er, And that wide riv - er is Jor - dan,

One more riv - er, There's one more riv - er to cross.—

4. The animals came four by four.
   One more river to cross.
   The hippopotamus got stuck in the door.
   One more river to cross.

5. The animals came five by five.
   One more river to cross.
   The bees came swarming from the hive.
   One more river to cross.

Look at the time signature. How many times will you tap in a measure?

10

Benediction, and glory, and wisdom, and thanksgiving, honor, and power, and strength to our God for ever and ever. Amen.

Apocalypse

Hymn to Christ the King

1. O King of Kings, let all a-dore, Al - le - lu - ia, al - le - lu - ia.
2. O Lord let all Thy peo-ple sing, Al - le - lu - ia, al - le - lu - ia.

We praise Thy name for ev - er more. Al - le - lu - ia, al - le - lu - ia.
Thee, Christ, we hail the na-tion's King. Al - le - lu - ia, al - le - lu - ia.

Tantum Ergo

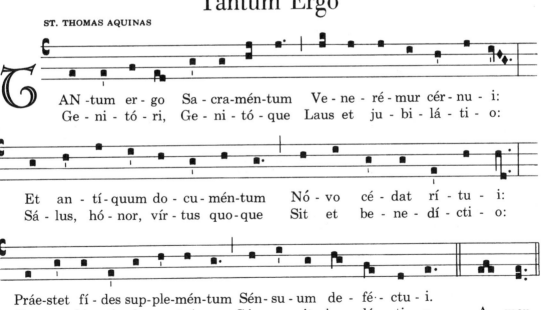

ST. THOMAS AQUINAS

AN -tum er - go Sa - cra-mén-tum   Ve - ne - ré - mur cér - nu - i:
Ge - ni - tó - ri, Ge - ni - tó - que   Laus et ju - bi - lá - ti - o:

Et an - tí - quum do - cu - mén-tum   Nó - vo cé - dat rí - tu - i:
Sá - lus, hó - nor, vír - tus quo-que   Sit et be - ne - dí - cti - o:

Práe-stet fí - des sup-ple-mén-tum Sén - su - um de - fé - ctu - i.
Pro - ce - dén - ti ab u - tró-que Cóm-par sit lau - dá - ti - o.   A - men.

This *neum* ¶◆ is a *climacus*.
The diamond-shaped notes are counted the same as square notes.
Where do you find *do* in this chant?
Can you name all the *neums* in this chant?

Gloria Patri

Gló - ri - a Pátri et Fílio, et Spi - rí - tu - i Sán - cto.

Sic - ut — érat in princípio, et núnc et sém - per, —

et — in — sáecula, sae - cu - ló-rum. A - men. —

Credo 1

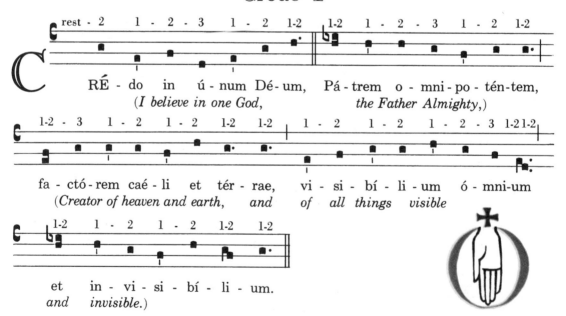

rest - 2 1 - 2 - 3 1 - 2 1-2 1-2 1 - 2 - 3 1 - 2 1-2

RÉ - do in ú - num Dé-um, Pá - trem o - mni - po - tén-tem,
(*I believe in one God,*   *the Father Almighty,*)

1-2 - 3 1 - 2 1 - 2 1-2 1-2 1 - 2 1 - 2 1 - 2 - 3 1-2 1-2

fa - ctó-rem caé - li et tér - rae, vi - si - bí - li - um ó - mni-um
(*Creator of heaven and earth,* *and* *of all things visible*

1-2 1 - 2 1 - 2 1-2 1-2

et in - vi - si - bí - li - um.
and invisible.)

Have you noticed that Gregorian chant never has a time signature? A time signature is used when music has *measured* rhythm. However, Gregorian chant has *free* rhythm. This means that the rhythm flows smoothly and evenly in pulses of twos and threes. The *ictus* mark, which looks like a small figure one (1) under a note, tells you where to begin a group of two or three pulses.

It will be interesting for a part of the class to count the pulses aloud as the remainder of the class sings the words.

March Along

WOLFGANG AMADEUS MOZART

March a - long and sing a song to - geth - er!

March a - long and sing a song to - geth - er!

Sun or rain, we nev - er mind the weath - er.

Sun or rain, we nev - er mind the weath - er.

In common time (C), be sure to count four steady beats in each measure.

Hail, King of Kings!

SISTER MARYANNA, O.P.

SISTER JOHN JOSEPH, C.S.J.

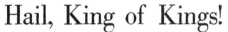

1. Hail, King of Kings! Hail, Prince of Peace! Our Eu - cha - ris - tic Lord! In
2. O Christ, our King, here car - ol - ing We pledge our youth to Thee. Great

heav-en served by an-gel hosts; On earth by men a-dored.
King di-vine, our hearts are Thine, In   lov-ing fe-al - ty.

This song is in the key of A flat.
Where is *do*?

13

The Marines' Hymn[1]

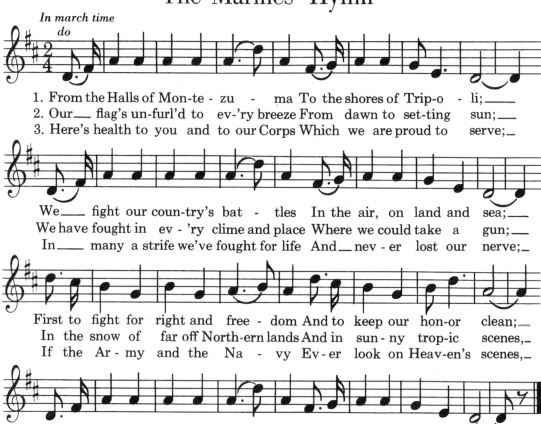

In march time

1. From the Halls of Mon-te - zu - ma To the shores of Trip-o - li;
2. Our flag's un-furl'd to ev-'ry breeze From dawn to set-ting sun;
3. Here's health to you and to our Corps Which we are proud to serve;

We fight our coun-try's bat - tles In the air, on land and sea;
We have fought in ev - 'ry clime and place Where we could take a gun;
In many a strife we've fought for life And nev - er lost our nerve;

First to fight for right and free - dom And to keep our hon-or clean;
In the snow of far off North-ern lands And in sun - ny trop-ic scenes,
If the Ar - my and the Na - vy Ev - er look on Heav-en's scenes,

We are proud to claim the ti - tle Of U - nit-ed States Ma - rines.
You will find us al - ways on the job, The U - nit-ed States Ma - rines.
They will find the streets are guard - ed By U - nit-ed States Ma - rines.

SEMPER FIDELIS

The Pledge of Allegiance

SISTER JOHN JOSEPH, C.S.J.

I pledge al-le-giance to the flag

Of the U - nit - ed States of A - mer - i - ca,

And to the Re-pub-lic for which it stands;

One na-tion un-der God,___ in - di-vis - i - ble,___

With lib - er - ty and jus - tice for all.

Prayer of Thanksgiving

DR. THEODORE BAKER

NETHERLANDS FOLK SONG

1. We gath-er to-geth-er to ask the Lord's bless-ing; He
2. Be-side us to guide us, our God with us join-ing, Or-
3. We all do ex-tol Thee, Thou lead-er in bat-tle, And

chas-tens and has-tens His will to make known; The
dain-ing, main-tain-ing His king-dom di-vine; So
pray that Thou still our De-fend-er wilt be. Let

wick-ed op-press-ing cease them___ from dis-tress-ing; Sing
from the be-gin-ning the fight___ we were win-ning; Thou,
Thy con-gre-ga-tion es-cape___ trib-u-la-tion; Thy

prais-es to His name, He for-gets not His own.
Lord, wast at our side, Let the glo-ry be Thine!
name be ev-er praised And Thy peo-ple be free!

Advent

O GOD, by whose word all things are sanctified, pour forth Thy blessing upon this wreath, and grant that we who use it may prepare our hearts for the coming of **CHRIST** and may receive from Thee abundant graces.

BLESSING OF THE ADVENT WREATH

Antiphon for Advent

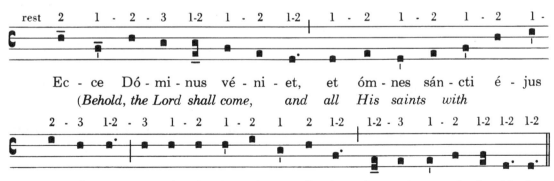

Ec - ce Dó - mi - nus vé - ni - et, et óm - nes sán - cti é - jus
(Behold, the Lord shall come, and all His saints with

cum é - o: et é - rit in dí - e íl - la lux má - gna, al - le - lú - ia.
Him; and there shall be in that day a great light.)

Some of you may count the rhythmic groups of twos and threes while the class sings the chant.

O Come, O Come, Emmanuel

1. O come, O come, Em-man - u - el,
2. O come, Thou Wis-dom from ___ on high,
3. O come, Thou Key of Da - vid, come

And ran-som cap-tive Is - ra - el
Who or-d'rest all things might - i - ly.
And o - pen wide our heav'n - ly home.

That mourns in lone - ly ex - ile here
To us the path of knowl - edge show,
Make straight the way to Heav - en's height,

Un - til the Son of God ___ ap - pear.
And teach us in her ways ___ to go.
And close the way to end - less night.

1,2,3. Re - joice! Re-joice! O Is - ra - el, To thee shall come E - man - u - el.

18

Come to My Window

JOSEPH DALY

SISTER ROSE MARGARET, C.S.J.

Come to my win-dow, oh, lad-die with me, And look at the stars that shine on the sea. There are two sil-ver stars far in the East. And the bright sil-ver moon hangs low in the west And our Fa-ther in Heav-en watch-es o'er all, The moon and the stars and the chil-dren small.

Hymn to Our Lady

Translated by SISTER M. LAURENT, C.S.J.

SPANISH FOLK SONG
SOUTHERN ARIZONA

1. The dawn is break-ing,__ and we a-wak-ing,__ Beg Ma-ry's lov-ing care,
2. When day has left us, __ and dark-ness bids us __ To close our eyes in sleep,

__ A - ve Ma - ri - a!   We ask her mer - cy____ and her pro -
__ A - ve Ma - ri - a!   We kneel and ask her __ that she, our

tec - tion,___ Her guid-ance ev - ’ry - where,___ A - ve Ma - ri - a.___
Moth- er, _____ Our souls and bod - ies keep, ___ A - ve Ma - ri - a.___

The Fisher Maiden

TRANSLATED BY CAROL FULLER

FRENCH FOLK SONG

Gracefully

1. "Come, pret-ty fish - er maid - en, Sail-ing your boat so free;___
2. "No, no, no, no!" she an - swers, "I need no lace at all. ___

Look where my cas - tle ris - es! Will you not mar - ry me?___
Look how the foam is weav - ing Pat-terns that rise and fall.___

Blos-soms I'll bring, fresh as the spring; Ru-bies, lac- es I'll buy,___
Sea-weeds that float close by my boat, Make a gar-den for me.___

Gifts that are glad sur - pris - es. No prince will be proud as I."___
I would not dream of leav - ing My home near the shin - ing sea."___

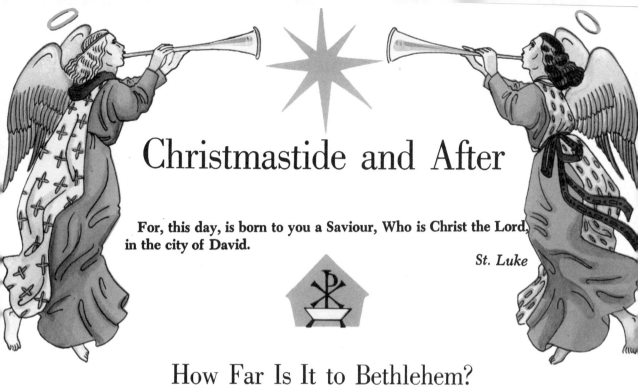

Christmastide and After

For, this day, is born to you a Saviour, Who is Christ the Lord, in the city of David.

St. Luke

How Far Is It to Bethlehem?

FRANCES CHESTERTON

OLD ENGLISH CAROL

1. How___ far is it to Beth - le - hem? Not ver - y far.
2. May___ we stroke the crea - tures there, Ox, ass, or sheep?

Shall___ we find the sta - ble room Lit by a star?
May___ we peek like them and see Je - sus a - sleep?

Can we see the lit - tle Child, Is He with - in?
If we touch His ti - ny hand, Will He a - wake?

If___ we lift the wood - en latch May we go in?
Will___ He know we've come so far Just for His sake?

21

Ecce Nomen Domini

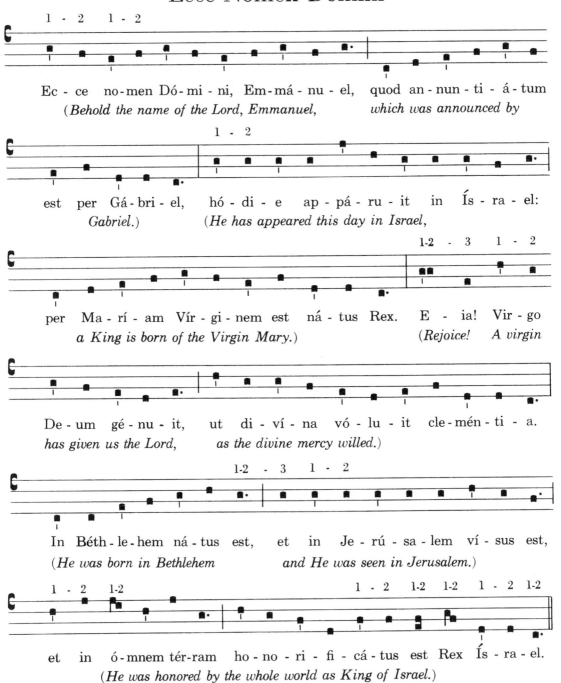

Ec - ce no - men Dó - mi - ni, Em - má - nu - el, quod an - nun - ti - á - tum
(*Behold the name of the Lord, Emmanuel,* *which was announced by*

est per Gá - bri - el, hó - di - e ap - pá - ru - it in Ís - ra - el:
Gabriel.) (*He has appeared this day in Israel,*

per Ma - rí - am Vír - gi - nem est ná - tus Rex. E - ia! Vir - go
a King is born of the Virgin Mary.) (*Rejoice!* *A virgin*

De - um gé - nu - it, ut di - ví - na vó - lu - it cle - mén - ti - a.
has given us the Lord, *as the divine mercy willed.*)

In Béth - le - hem ná - tus est, et in Je - rú - sa - lem ví - sus est,
(*He was born in Bethlehem* *and He was seen in Jerusalem.*)

et in ó - mnem tér - ram ho - no - ri - fi - cá - tus est Rex Ís - ra - el.
(*He was honored by the whole world as King of Israel.*)

Sing the count of this chant to its melody. All the difficult places are marked
for you.

Puer Natus

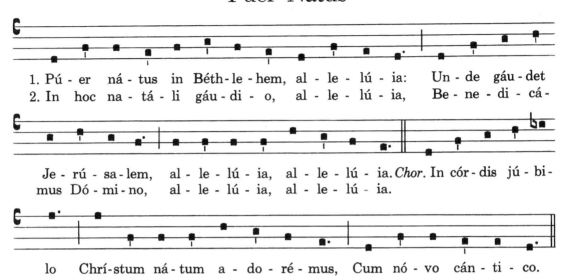

1. Pú - er ná - tus in Béth - le - hem, al - le - lú - ia: Un - de gáu - det
2. In hoc na - tá - li gáu - di - o, al - le - lú - ia, Be - ne - di - cá -

Je - rú - sa - lem, al - le - lú - ia, al - le - lú - ia. *Chor.* In cór - dis jú - bi -
mus Dó - mi - no, al - le - lú - ia, al - le - lú - ia.

lo Chrí - stum ná - tum a - do - ré - mus, Cum nó - vo cán - ti - co.

Count out the rhythmic groups in this chant.
This is a flat (♭). It changes *ti* to *te*.

Child's Christmas Carol

SISTER MARIS STELLA, C.S.J.   SISTER JOHN JOSEPH, C.S.J.

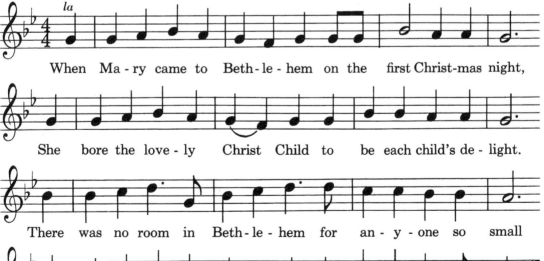

When Ma - ry came to Beth - le - hem on the first Christ - mas night,

She bore the love - ly Christ Child to be each child's de - light.

There was no room in Beth - le - hem for an - y - one so small

And yet so great as Ma - ry's Child but in an ox - en stall.

23

Shepherd, Tell Us

GRETCHEN MURRAY   FRENCH-CANADIAN FOLK TUNE

1. Shep - herd, shep-herd, tell us, What can be ___
2. In a low - ly man - ger, Ly - ing there, ___

Yon - der in the sta - ble Where a light we see?
Sleeps the lit - tle Christ Child, Sweet and fresh and fair.

Christ Is Born

S. R. M.   POLISH FOLK TUNE

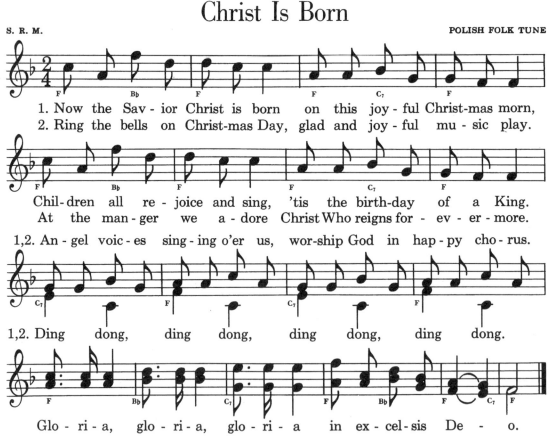

1. Now the Sav - ior Christ is born on this joy - ful Christ-mas morn,
2. Ring the bells on Christ-mas Day, glad and joy - ful mu - sic play.

Chil - dren all re - joice and sing, 'tis the birth-day of a King.
At the man - ger we a - dore Christ Who reigns for - ev - er - more.

1,2. An - gel voic - es sing - ing o'er us, wor-ship God in hap - py cho - rus.

1,2. Ding dong, ding dong, ding dong, ding dong.

Glo - ri - a, glo - ri - a, glo - ri - a in ex - cel - sis De - o.

24

He Is Born, the Holy Child

Translated by SUSANNA MYERS

FRENCH CAROL

He is born, the— Ho-ly Child,— Or-gan, flute, sweet mu-sic play!—

He is born, the— Ho-ly Child, Praise Him, all, this Christ-mas Day.

1. Look! He lies in a man-ger bed, He, the King of— heav'n-ly glo-ry,
2. In the sky bright an-gels sing, Bring-ing us the Christ-mas sto-ry,
3. With the shep-herds and the kings, Let us kneel in — love and won-der,

Fair and soft is the Ba-by head, Cra-dled there in the man-ger bed;—
Dis-tant ech-oes— joy-ful ring; Peace, good will, the— an-gels sing;—
Ask-ing hum-bly— for His bless-ing, For all chil-dren— as they sing;—

25

TRANSLATED   POLISH CAROL

GROUP 1

1. "Come, shep-herds, to a - dore Christ, our Sav - ior. Where, tell us, where?"
2. "Where shall we find the Child in the man - ger. Where, tell us, where?"
3. "Who kneels be - side His poor lit - tle cra - dle. Who, tell us, who?"
4. "Who guards the Ba - by, keeps Him from dan - ger. Who, tell us, who?"

GROUP 2

"Laid in a man - ger bed in the town of Beth - le - hem."
"There in a sta - ble cave in the town of Beth - le - hem."
"Ma - ry, His Moth - er fair, in the town of Beth - le - hem."
"Jo - seph, the val - iant one, in the town of Beth - le - hem."

St. Joseph's Vigil

DENIS McCARTHY   JAN BEZDEK

1. Si - lent - ly, with fold - ed hands, By the man - ger Jo - seph stands,
2. Ar - ti - san to whom is giv'n Know-ledge of the things of heav'n;

O'er the In - fant in the straw, Watch-ing with a ho - ly awe,
Low - ly one who knows and sees God's e - ter - nal mys - ter - ies.

Guard-ian of the Moth - er mild, Guard-ian of the Ho - ly Child.
Guard-ian of the Moth - er mild, Guard-ian of the Ho - ly Child.

26

Christmas Lullaby

English version by
CHRISTINE TURNER CURTIS

POLISH FOLK TUNE

Gently

1. Loo - lull - a - by, Je - su, and safe be Thy___ sleep - ing;
2. Loo - lull - a - by, Je - su, our car - ols we___ sing Thee;

Near Thee is Thy Moth - er, Her still vig - il keep - ing.
Loaves made of fine wheat and ripe ber - ries we bring Thee.

Thou art like a star ev - er - more the heav - ens a - dorn - ing.
Down come snow - y an - gels Thy ho - ly cra - dle at - tend - ing,

Thou art the white rose - bud that o - pens at morn - ing.
Loo - lull - a - by, Je - su, till night - time is end - ing.

If the last flat is *fa*, where will you find *do*?

CHRISTMAS IN MEXICO

The Players

NARRATOR	JUAN
TERESITA, a little Mexican girl	JOSÉ
SEÑORA MEDINA, her mother	MANUELITO
SEÑOR GARCIA, a neighbor	ROSA
SEÑORA GARCIA, his wife	CHORUS

JUAN, JOSÉ, MANUELITO — Children

NARRATOR. We are in a little village in Mexico. Teresita Medina, a little Mexican girl, is getting ready to join a *posada*, a Christmas procession. She is wearing her best clothes and is very much excited.

TERESITA. O Mamacita, look at my dress. Is it all right? I want to look my best for the procession tonight.

SEÑORA MEDINA. It is beautiful, Teresita. Now, here is your candle. You must hurry, for I hear the children coming down the street.

(*While* TERESITA *lights her candle, music is heard in the distance.* CHORUS *hums or sings softly the carol* "*Looking for a Lodging.*")

TERESITA. Good night, Mamacita.

SEÑORA MEDINA. Good night, Teresita. Remember it is an honor to carry a candle before the Infant.

TERESITA. I shall remember, Mamacita. (*She goes out to join a small procession of children carrying lighted candles. Two boys carry a litter, upon which is a small Christmas stable with little figures of the Infant Jesus, Mary, and Joseph.*)

28

(The children walk slowly, singing:)

Looking for a Lodging

After the original

TRADITIONAL MEXICAN CAROL

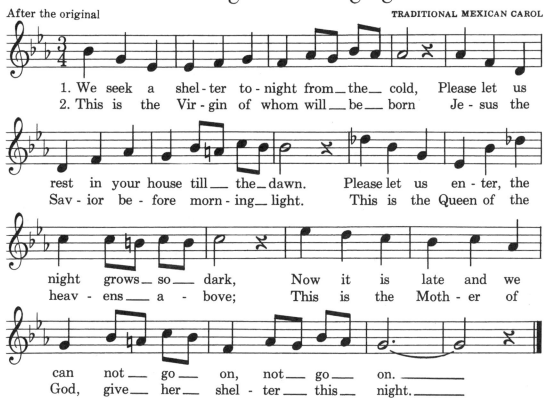

1. We seek a shel-ter to-night from the cold, Please let us
2. This is the Vir-gin of whom will be born Je-sus the

rest in your house till the dawn. Please let us en-ter, the
Sav-ior be-fore morn-ing light. This is the Queen of the

night grows so dark, Now it is late and we
heav-ens a-bove; This is the Moth-er of

can not go on, not go on.
God, give her shel-ter this night.

(At the end of the song one of the boys knocks on a door.)

JUAN. *(Knocking again.)* Señor Garcia! We come to seek lodging.
Open to us, please! We bring the Holy Infant, and His
mother Mary, and the good Saint Joseph!

SEÑOR GARCIA. Come, children; the Holy Infant is welcome to my house. There are gifts and good things for those who bring Him here. (*The children enter the house and the boys place the litter on a table. Then all join in a song.*)

A la ru

Translated by
SISTER M. LAURENT, C.S.J.

SPANISH FOLK SONG from ARIZONA

1. "Go to sleep, Lit-tle Je-sus." Ma - ry soft - ly sings to you.___
2. An - gels hov-er a-round you, Shep-herds look with won-der too.___

Ev - er so gen-tly she rocks you As she sings to you, a___ la ru.
Ma - ry so lov-ing-ly guards you As she sings to you, a___ la ru.

CHORUS

A la ru_____ a la me,_____ A la ru_____

a la me,_____ A la ru, a la me, a la ru._____

SEÑOR GARCIA. Now, children, look at the fine *piñata* we have ready
       for you. It is filled with gifts and candy, and you must all
       take your turn trying to break it. Then all it holds will be
       yours. Who wants to try first?

ALL THE CHILDREN. José! He is the biggest. He will surely break it!

SEÑOR GARCIA. Come, José, let me blindfold you. Now I will turn
       you around and around, and then we shall see if you can
       find the *piñata*. Here is your stick; now break the *piñata*
       for us.

CHILDREN. (*Excitedly*) Above your head, José! Oh, no, you are not
       near it now. Go to the left! Hold the stick higher. (JOSÉ
       tries valiantly, but does not succeed.)

SEÑORA GARCIA. Someone else must try, since José cannot find the
       piñata. Come, Manuelito, you shall be next. (MANUELITO
       *also tries, waving the stick wildly, while the children call
       directions. He cannot find the piñata.*)

SEÑORA GARCIA. If the boys cannot find it, we must let a girl try.

SEÑORA GARCIA. Rosa, will you try?

ROSA. I shall try, Señora Garcia. When I find the *piñata* with my stick
       I shall hit it hard and break it, and we shall have the candy.
       (ROSA *tries to find the piñata, but without success.*)

SEÑOR GARCIA. Let us try the smallest child. Teresita, my little one,
       let me blindfold you now.

TERESITA. Oh, it is so dark with my eyes covered!

SEÑOR GARCIA. Go a little to your right, Teresita, and hold the stick
       higher. There! You have found it. Now hit it hard.
       (TERESITA *strikes the piñata, which breaks and scatters gifts
       and candy upon the children.*)

ALL THE CHILDREN. She broke it, she broke it! Teresita broke the
       piñata! (*They scramble for the candy and gifts.*)

SEÑOR GARCIA. (*Laughing*) Well, my little ones, you did very well. Now, gather up your gifts, children. Your parents are waiting for you. It is bed time.

SEÑORA GARCIA. And before you go we shall sing another hymn to the Holy Infant.

Lullaby to the Infant Jesus

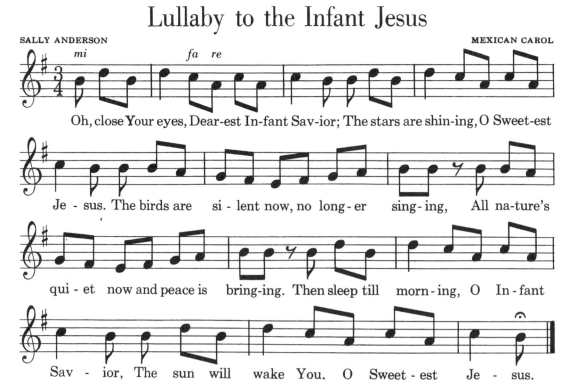

SALLY ANDERSON   MEXICAN CAROL

Oh, close Your eyes, Dear-est In-fant Sav-ior; The stars are shin-ing, O Sweet-est Je-sus. The birds are si-lent now, no long-er sing-ing, All na-ture's qui-et now and peace is bring-ing. Then sleep till morn-ing, O In-fant Sav-ior, The sun will wake You, O Sweet-est Je-sus.

(The children take up the litter and go out singing.)

Glory to God

Translated by
SISTER M. LAURENT, C.S.J.

SPANISH FOLK SONG

1. "Glo - ry   be to God in the high-est," sang the an-gels to the shep-herds.
2. "You will find the Child in the man-ger," sang the an-gels to the shep-herds.

"Go to Beth-le-hem's lit-tle sta - ble,   go as fast as you are a - ble."
"He has brought to us our sal - va - tion,   He, the hope of ev - 'ry   na-tion."

CHORUS

Hur - ry, hur - ry, shep - herds, has - ten to a - dore

Je - sus Christ, the In - fant King of   heav'n and   earth.

Hur - ry then and thank Him for His   hum - ble   birth.

Deck the Hall

OLD WELSH AIR

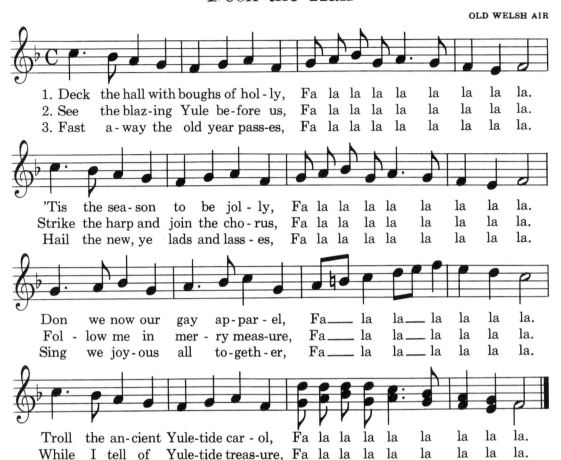

1. Deck the hall with boughs of hol-ly, Fa la la la la la la la la.
2. See the blaz-ing Yule be-fore us, Fa la la la la la la la la.
3. Fast a-way the old year pass-es, Fa la la la la la la la la.

'Tis the sea-son to be jol-ly, Fa la la la la la la la la.
Strike the harp and join the cho-rus, Fa la la la la la la la la.
Hail the new, ye lads and lass-es, Fa la la la la la la la la.

Don we now our gay ap-par-el, Fa___ la la___ la la la la.
Fol-low me in mer-ry meas-ure, Fa___ la la___ la la la la.
Sing we joy-ous all to-geth-er, Fa___ la la___ la la la la.

Troll the an-cient Yule-tide car-ol, Fa la la la la la la la la.
While I tell of Yule-tide treas-ure, Fa la la la la la la la la.
Heed-less of the wind and weath-er, Fa la la la la la la la la.

Old Irish Prayer

From the OLD IRISH
by THOMAS WALSH

MARYBETH BAYLEY

May the sweet Name of Je-sus be lov-ing-ly grav-en On my heart's in-most ha-ven,

O___ Ma-ry, my Moth-er, Be Je-sus my Broth-er, And ___ I, Je-sus' broth-er!

A bind - ing of love that no dis - tance can sev - er,

Be be - tween us for - ev - er, O my Sav - ior for - ev - er!

The Juniper Tree

EILEEN DUGGAN

SISTER JOHN JOSEPH, C.S.J.

1. Who does not love_____ the ju - ni - per tree?
2. Jo - seph and Ma - ry and lit - tle wee Son,

The scent of its branch - es comes back to me,
Came_____ to rest when the day was done!

And_____ ev - er I think of the Ho - ly Three
And the lit - tle Child slept on His Moth - er's knee

Who_____ came to rest by the ju - ni - per tree!
In the shel - ter sweet of the ju - ni - per tree.

Lullaby

NORWEGIAN

Sleep, lit - tle Ka - ri, sleep while you may; Shad-ows are fall-ing, gone is the day,

Lull - a - by, ___ lull - a - by, Lull - a - by, ___ lull - a - by,

Noth-ing will harm you, moth-er is here; Sweet dreams be with you, sleep, Ka-ri dear.

Lull - a - by, ___ lull - a - by, Lull - a - by, Lull - a - by.

Dormi, Non Piángere

ITALIAN FOLK SONG

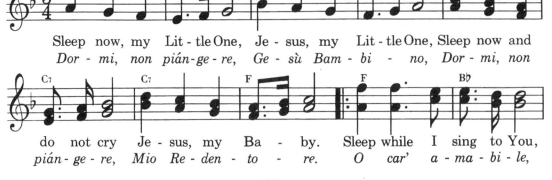

Sleep now, my Lit - tle One, Je - sus, my Lit - tle One, Sleep now and
Dor - mi, non pián - ge - re, Ge - sù Bam - bi - no, Dor - mi, non

do not cry Je - sus, my Ba - by. Sleep while I sing to You,
pián - ge - re, Mio Re - den - to - re. O car' a - ma - bi - le,

36

Tell you I love You, An - gels from Heav - en
Ge - sù Bam - bi - no, A - mor di - vi - no,

Hov - er a - bove___You. bove You.
ac - cend' il co - re. co - re.

English Lullaby

J. MEDAILLE

GILES FARNABY

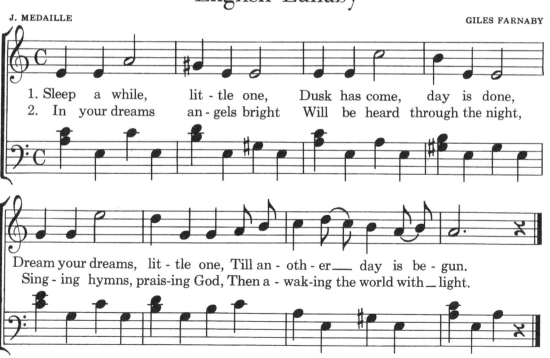

1. Sleep a while, lit - tle one, Dusk has come, day is done,
2. In your dreams an - gels bright Will be heard through the night,

Dream your dreams, lit - tle one, Till an - oth - er___ day is be - gun.
Sing - ing hymns, prais - ing God, Then a - wak - ing the world with___ light.

Shoo Fly

AMERICAN SINGING GAME

*Single circles, of not more than eight to a circle, with hands joined.
It is important that hands be joined firmly throughout the game.*

Shoo fly, don't both-er me, Shoo fly, don't both-er me.

Move forward, swinging arms upward to form a "teepee." *Move backward, swinging arms downward.*

Shoo fly, don't both-er me, For I be-long to some-bod-y. I

Repeat first action. *Repeat second action.*

do, I do, I do, And I will not tell you who; For

*One couple form arch. Couple opposite arch lead group through it
until the circle is turned inside out. On repeat, reverse action.*

I be-long to some-bod-y, Yes, in-deed I do. I do.

38

Billy Boy

MOUNTAIN FOLK SONG

Gaily

1. Oh,___ where__ have you been, Bil - ly Boy, Bil - ly Boy?
2. Did she ask you to come in, Bil - ly Boy, Bil - ly Boy?
3. Did she set for you a chair, Bil - ly Boy, Bil - ly Boy?
4. Can she bake a cher - ry pie, Bil - ly Boy, Bil - ly Boy?

Oh,___ where__ have you been, charm - ing Bil - ly?___
Did she ask you to come in, charm - ing Bil - ly?___
Did she set for you a chair, charm - ing Bil - ly?___
Can she bake a cher - ry pie, charm - ing Bil - ly?___

I have been to seek a wife, She's the joy__ of my life,
Yes, she asked me to come in, With a dim-ple in her chin,
Yes, she set for me a chair, She has ring-lets in her hair,
She can bake a cher - ry pie, Quick's a cat can wink her eye,

1,2,3,4. She's a young thing and can - not leave her moth - er.___

Dixie

DAN D. EMMETT

Quickly

1. I___ wish I was___ in the land of cot-ton, Old times there___ are
2. There buck-wheat cakes and___ In-dian bat-ter Make you fat or a

not for-got-ten, Look a - way! Look a - way! Look a - way! Dix-ie
lit - tle fat-ter, Look a - way! Look a - way! Look a - way! Dix-ie

Land! In___ Dix-ie Land where I was born___ Ear-ly on one
Land! Then hoe it down and scratch your grav-el, to Dix-ie's Land I'm

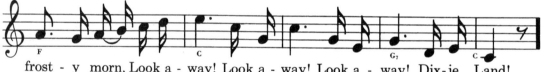

frost - y morn, Look a - way! Look a - way! Look a - way! Dix-ie Land!
bound to trav-el, Look a - way! Look a - way! Look a - way! Dix-ie Land!

CHORUS

Then I wish I was in Dix - ie, Hoo-ray! (hoo-ray) Hoo-ray! (hoo-ray)
do . . . . fa . . . . re . . . . so . . . . .

In Dix - ie Land I'll take my stand To live and die in Dix - ie,
do . . . . fa . . . . do . . . . so . . . .

A - way, (a-way) a - way, (a-way) A - way down South in Dix - ie,
do . . . . . so . . . . do . . . . do . . .

A - way, (a-way) a - way, (a-way) A - way down South in Dix - ie.
do . . . . . so . . . . do . . . . so . . do

The Patriots

Adapted by JANE B. WALTERS

THURINGIAN FOLK SONG

1. 'Tis here we are pledg - ing with heart and with hand,
2. Now all join the chor - us, let un - ion a - bide,
3. O star - ry Old Glo - ry of red, white and blue!

Full meas - ure of de - vo - tion to thee, our native land;
The flag is wav - ing o'er us for which our fa - thers died;
We love thy hon - ored sto - ry; to thee we'll e'er be true;

Full meas - ure of de - vo - tion to thee, our na - tive land.
The flag is wav - ing o'er us for which our fa - thers died.
We love thy hon - ored sto - ry; to thee we'll e'er be true.

Where is *do* in the key of F?

From *The Golden Book of Favorite Songs*, Copyright 1923–1951 by Hall &
McCreary Company. Used by permission.

Lumen ad Revelationem

Lú - men* ad re - ve - la - ti - ó - nem gén - ti - um: et gló - ri - am
(*A light to the revelation of the Gentiles and the glory*

plé - bis tú - ae Ís - ra - el.
of Thy people Israel.)

Gló - ri - a Pá - tri et Fí - li - o* et Spi - rí - tu - i Sán - cto. *Repeat Lumen.*

Sic - ut é - rat in prin - cí - pi - o, et nunc, et sem - per,*

et in saé - cu - la sae - cu - ló - rum. A - men. *Repeat Lumen.*

When the Blessèd Virgin and St. Joseph took the Infant Jesus to the temple to present Him to the Lord, a saintly old man named Simeon took the Child in his arms and sang a canticle of praise and thanksgiving. He was grateful that he had been given the grace of seeing the Saviour.

This short chant is part of Simeon's canticle. Ask your teacher to tell you the story.

Hymn to St. John the Baptist

do

Ut qué - ant lá - xis re - so - ná - re fí - bris

Mí - ra ge - stó - rum fá - mu - li tu - ó - rum,

Sól - ve pol - lú - ti lá - bi - i re - á - tum,

Sán - cte Jo - an - nes.

Our music syllables come from this hymn. If you take the note above each italicized syllable and put it on a staff you will have most of the scale.

Ut re mi fa so la

The syllable *Ut* is hard to sing, so it has been changed to *Do*, the first syllable of the word *Dominus* (Lord).

Do re mi fa so la ti do

If you write this scale on a modern five-line staff it looks like this:

Do re mi fa so la ti do

This is the F Major scale. *Do* is in the first space, as it is in the Gregorian staff. Ask your teacher to tell you the story of Guido d'Arezzo and the music syllables.

43

The Star-Spangled Banner

FRANCIS SCOTT KEY

JOHN STAFFORD SMITH

1. Oh,___ say! can you see,___ by the dawn's ear - ly light,
2. On the shore, dim - ly seen_ through the mists of the deep,
3. Oh,___ thus be it ev - er when___ free - men shall stand

What so proud - ly we hailed at the twi - light's last gleam - ing,
Where the foe's haugh - ty host in dread si - lence re - pos - es,
Be - tween their loved homes and the war's des - o - la - tion!

Whose broad stripes and bright stars, through the per - il - ous fight,
What is that which the breeze, o'er the tow - er - ing steep,
Blest with vic - t'ry and peace, may the heav'n - res - cued land

O'er the ram - parts we watched were so gal - lant - ly stream - ing?
As it fit - ful - ly blows, half con - ceals, half dis - clos - es?
Praise the Pow'r that hath made and pre - served us a na - tion!

And the rock - ets' red glare, the bombs burst - ing in air,
Now it catch - es the gleam of the morn - ing's first beam,
Then___ con - quer we must, when our cause it is just,

Gave___ proof through the night___ that our flag was still there.
In full glo - ry re - flect - ed now___ shines on the stream;
And___ this be our mot - to: "In___ God is our trust!"

Oh,___ say does that___ Star-Span-gled Ban-ner___ yet___ wave___
'Tis the Star-Span-gled___ Ban-ner, oh, long may_ it ___ wave___
And the Star-Span-gled ___ Ban-ner in tri-umph shall___ wave___

O'er the land___ of the free and the home of the brave?
O'er the land___ of the free and the home of the brave!
O'er the land___ of the free and the home of the brave!

America

SAMUEL FRANCIS SMITH   TRADITIONAL

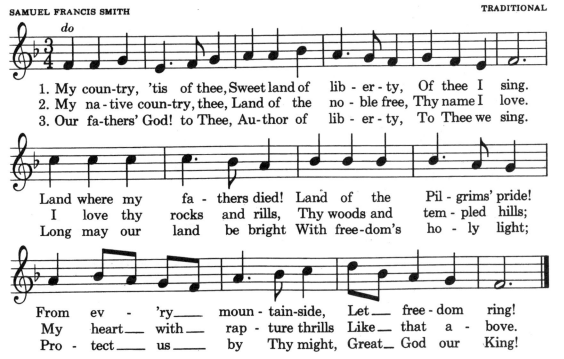

1. My coun-try, 'tis of thee, Sweet land of lib-er-ty, Of thee I sing.
2. My na-tive coun-try, thee, Land of the no-ble free, Thy name I love.
3. Our fa-thers' God! to Thee, Au-thor of lib-er-ty, To Thee we sing.

Land where my fa-thers died! Land of the Pil-grims' pride!
I love thy rocks and rills, Thy woods and tem-pled hills;
Long may our land be bright With free-dom's ho-ly light;

From ev-'ry___ moun-tain-side, Let___ free-dom ring!
My heart___ with___ rap-ture thrills Like___ that a-bove.
Pro-tect___ us___ by Thy might, Great_ God our King!

Away down South [1]

SOUTHERN FOLK TUNE

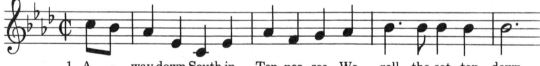

1. A - way down South in Ten-nes - see, We roll the cot - ton down,
2. Oh,— hoist that bale and sing this song, We roll the cot - ton down,

A - way down South in Ten-nes-see, We roll the cot-ton down, We roll the cot-ton down,
Oh, hoist that bale and sing this song, We roll the cot-ton down, We roll the cot-ton down,

We roll the cot-ton down. A- way down South in Ten-nes-see, We roll the cot-ton down.
We roll the cot-ton down, Oh, hoist that bale and sing this song, We roll the cot-ton down.

Find *do* from the key signature.

[1] By permission of the copyright owners, Boosey & Hawkes.

Lent and Passiontide

**O Lord, remember not against us the iniquities of the past;
may Your compassion quickly come to us.**

Stabat Mater

1. Stá - bat Má - ter do - lo - ró - sa   Jux - ta crú - cem la - cri - mó - sa,
2. Cú - jus á - ni-mam ge - mén-tem,   Con - tri - stá - tam et do - lén - tem
3. Quae moe - ré - bat, et do - lé - bat   Pi - a Má - ter, dum vi - dé - bat

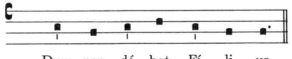

Dum pen - dé - bat Fí - li - us.
Per - trans - í - vit glá - di - us.
Na - ti poe - nas ín - cly - ti.

1. *At the cross her station keeping,*
   Stood the mournful Mother weeping,
   Close to Jesus to the last.

2. *Through her heart, His sorrow sharing,*
   All His bitter anguish bearing,
   Now at length the sword has passed.

3. *Christ above in torment hangs:*
   She beneath beholds the pangs
   Of her dying glorious Son.

Sing the hymn all the way through while you count the pulses.
Remember to begin with "rest-two", since the second note has an ictus under it.

Mary at the Cross
Estaba al pie de la Cruz

SPANISH FOLK SONG

'Neath the Cross her vig - il keep - ing,
Es - ta - ba al pie de__ la Cruz__

Stood the Vir - gin Moth - er weep - ing,
la Ma - dre__ de gra - cia her - mo - sa,

Sad was she and sore__ af - flict - ed
a - fli - gi - da y do - lo - ro - sa,

Thus to see__ her Je - sus dy - ing,
vien - do pen - dien - te a Je - sús,__

Thus to see__ her Je - sus dy - ing.
vien - do pen - dien - te a__ Je - sús.__

La-do-mi is as important in minor keys as *do-mi-so* is in major keys.

St. Patrick's Day

SISTER M. LAURENT, C.S.J.

IRISH FOLK TUNE

1. Oh, the sham-rocks will ap-pear for 'tis St. Pat-rick's Day,
2. 'Tis a day for cel-e-brat-ing, 'tis St. Pat-rick's Day.

And the flags will wave, the band will play, we'll all be gay.
Lads and lass-ies are all wait-ing for the band to play.

CHORUS

Dance a jig and sing a song, let laugh-ter ring the whole day long.

Hearts are light and eyes are bright for 'tis St. Pat-rick's Day,

Hearts are light and eyes are bright for 'tis St. Pat-rick's Day.

In this song there are two typical rhythm patterns in $\frac{6}{8}$ time.

Notice how they are counted:

My Goose

ROUND

Why does-n't my goose sing as well as thy goose,

When I paid for my goose twice as much as thine?

49

St. Joseph, a man beloved of God and men, whose memory is benediction.

O Spouse of Heaven's Queen

TRADITIONAL

1. O spouse of heav-en's queen all fair, God chose thee as no oth-er,
2. Thou guard-ian of our Church so vast, Her sol - ace and pro - tec-tion;

To guide and guard with lov - ing care, The Word's own spot-less Moth-er.
On thee our trust-ing hope is cast, Oh, grant us thy di - rec-tion.

Thou dost be-hold her near His throne A-dorned with scep-tre and with crown.
May young and old, may all man-kind In thy loved care sal - va - tion find.

St. Jo-seph in __ each need-y __ hour, Pro-tect us by thy might-y pow'r.
St. Jo-seph in __ each need-y __ hour, Pro-tect us by thy might-y pow'r.

Ave Maria

EARLY ENGLISH ROUND

A - ve Ma-rí - a, grá - ti-a ple - na, Dó-mi-nus te - cum.

Grant, we beseech Thee, O Lord, that the power of the Holy Spirit may abide in us. May it mercifully cleanse our hearts and defend us from all danger.

Old English Prayer

OLD ENGLISH

SISTER CECILIA, S.C.

Mat-thew, Mark, Luke, and John, Bless the bed that I lie on.

Be - fore I lay me down to sleep, I give my soul to Christ to keep.

Four cor - ners to my bed, Four an - gels there a - spread.

Two to foot and two to head, And two to car-ry me when I'm dead.

If an - y dan - ger come to me, Sweet Je - sus Christ de - liv - er me!

And if I die be - fore I wake, I pray that Christ my soul will take!

I should like to know, Old Black Crow!

I know, I know, I know, Old Black Crow!

Gloria, Laus, et Honor

Gló - ri - a, laus, et hó - nor, tí - bi sit Rex Chrí - ste Red - ém - ptor:
(Glory, praise and honor be to Thee,   Christ, Redeemer, King,

Cú - i pu - e - rí - le dé - cus próm-psit Ho - sán - na pí - um.
to Whom the children sang their glad hosannas.)

Count the rhythmic groups of twos and threes. The first note of a neum is "one" and begins a rhythmic group. When two notes are close together, like this ( ) the first one receives the *ictus*.

A Bird in a Tree

TRANSLATED

GERMAN FOLK SONG

Gaily

1. A lit - tle bird sat in a tree And sang a cheer-ful mel - o - dy,
2. He sang for wife and chil-dren three So safe - ly nest - ed in the tree,
3. And when his tune-ful song was done, He chirped and sang an - oth - er one;

1,2,3. Tir-ra li li li, Tir-ra li li li, Tir-ra li li li li lay.

52

FRANZ SCHUBERT

Franz Peter Schubert, who was the thirteenth child in a family of fourteen children, was born on the outskirts of Vienna on January 31, 1797. He was baptized in his church on the following day.

Schubert, whose father was a schoolmaster and strongly devoted to his children, came from a poor but very musical family. When Franz was only three years old he could pick out on the piano tunes he heard in the little family concerts at home. His father gave him lessons on the violin; his eldest brother, Ignatius, taught him to play the piano.

At church Franz was always interested in the choirboys. He loved the beautiful singing at the High Masses and wanted very much to be one of the choir members. When Schubert was only eight years old the choirmaster admitted him to the choir. In fact, the master was delighted to have such a beautiful singer in the group. He was surprised at the ease with which young Schubert could sing the difficult songs and Masses. He was a better sight reader than many of the older boys. The choirmaster was amused, too, at Schubert's hearty appetite, for like other boys of his age he was always hungry.

While Franz was a member of this choir he studied violin, viola, organ, and piano. His school work, however, was not neglected, for he also had to study reading, geography, arithmetic, history, poetry, French, and Italian. He spoke German in his home and at school.

Schubert was well liked because he was good-natured and lively. One of his close friends said that he was an honest, simple-hearted person whom one could not help loving. His faith in God was never shaken.

Schubert was always poor. During the last four years of his life he became weaker and tired easily, probably because of a life of hardship. He was only thirty-one years old when he died.

The world will always remember Franz Schubert for the many beautiful songs he wrote, the type that all people like. He also wrote symphonies, of which the *Unfinished Symphony* is the best known, pieces for the piano and other instruments, and very many other musical works.

Slumber Song

ANONYMOUS

FRANZ SCHUBERT

1. Slum-ber sweet-ly, slum-ber, O__ my__ ba-by; O'er thy cra-dle
2. Eve-ning shad-ows call thee now to__ slum-ber; Close a-round thee

moth-er watch will keep. In the morn-ing, when the__ sun is
is thy moth-er's arm. Fond-est wish-es, thoughts most sweet and

shin-ing, Thou shalt wak-en from thy gen-tle sleep.
ten-der, All will shield thee, dear-est child, from harm.

Moon of Silver White

CHRISTINE TURNER CURTIS

FRANZ SCHUBERT

Adagio cantabile

1. "Tell me, tell me, moon of sil-ver white, Through my cham-ber win-dow peep-ing,
2. "Tell me, tell me, moon of sil-ver white, Through my cham-ber win-dow beam-ing,

Why you wan-der in the lone-ly night, When all folk be-low are sleep-ing?"
Why you wake me in the lone-ly night, With your glanc-es soft-ly stream-ing?"

"When the twi-light fades from the skies, When the lil - ies close their dream-y eyes,
"When the shad-ows dark-en and fall, When the night en-folds the ma-ples tall,

Through the dusk-y for-est, soft-ly I a-rise; O-ver all that live my vig-il keep-ing."
Safe-ly I will guard you, watch-ing o-ver all; Hold you in my care, a-sleep and dream-ing."

The Wind

HENRY JOHNSTONE

Arranged from DESMARET

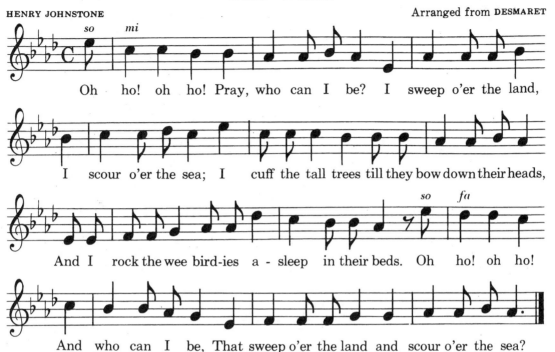

so mi

Oh ho! oh ho! Pray, who can I be? I sweep o'er the land,

I scour o'er the sea; I cuff the tall trees till they bow down their heads,

And I rock the wee bird-ies a - sleep in their beds. Oh ho! oh ho!

so fa

And who can I be, That sweep o'er the land and scour o'er the sea?

Find *do* from the key signature. Remember that *so-mi* and *so-fa* do not sound
the same.

In the Lord's Atoning Grief

ST. BONAVENTURE
TRANSLATED

17th CENTURY HYMN

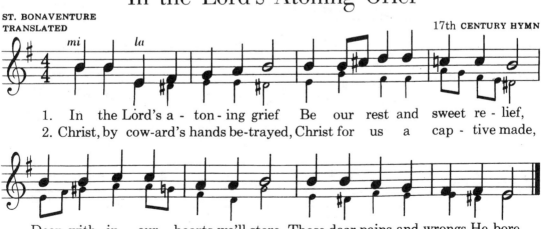

mi   la

1. In the Lord's a - ton - ing grief Be our rest and sweet re - lief,
2. Christ, by cow-ard's hands be-trayed, Christ for us a cap - tive made,

Deep with-in our hearts we'll store Those dear pains and wrongs He bore.
Christ up - on the bit - ter tree, Slain by man, all praise to Thee.

55

All Night, All Day

SPIRITUAL

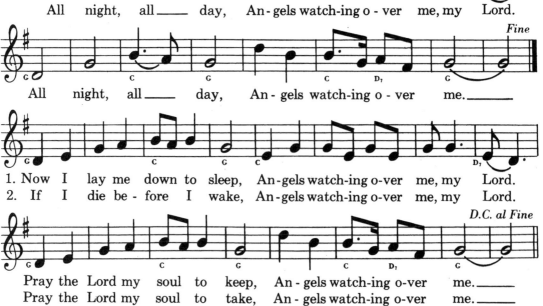

All night, all____ day, An-gels watch-ing o-ver me, my Lord.

Fine

All night, all____ day, An-gels watch-ing o-ver me.____

1. Now I lay me down to sleep, An-gels watch-ing o-ver me, my Lord.
2. If I die be-fore I wake, An-gels watch-ing o-ver me, my Lord.

D.C. al Fine

Pray the Lord my soul to keep, An-gels watch-ing o-ver me.____
Pray the Lord my soul to take, An-gels watch-ing o-ver me.____

Eastertide

**Christ rises resplendent, may His light
Dispel from heart and mind the evil night.**

Christ Is Risen

TRADITIONAL
Arranged

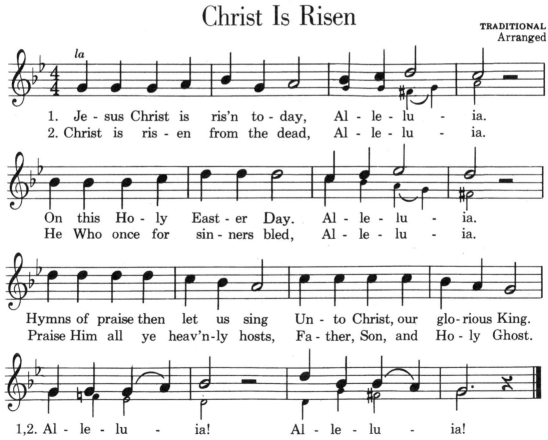

1. Je - sus Christ is ris'n to - day, Al - le - lu - ia.
2. Christ is ris - en from the dead, Al - le - lu - ia.

On this Ho - ly East - er Day. Al - le - lu - ia.
He Who once for sin - ners bled, Al - le - lu - ia.

Hymns of praise then let us sing Un - to Christ, our glo - rious King.
Praise Him all ye heav'n - ly hosts, Fa - ther, Son, and Ho - ly Ghost.

1,2. Al - le - lu - ia! Al - le - lu - ia!

Antiphon for Easter Vigil

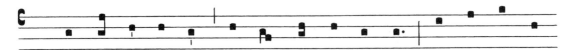

Et val - de ma - ne ú - na sab - ba - tó - rum, vé - ni - unt ad
(*And very early in the morning, the first day of the week, they came*

mo - nu - mén - tum, ór - to jam só - le, al - le - lú - ia:
to the sepulchre, the sun being now risen.)

Where is *do* in this chant?
What is the first syllable?

Ho! Every Sleeper, Waken!

1. Ho! Ev - 'ry sleep - er, wak - en! The sun is in the sky.

2. A - wak - en, a - wak - en And hear the cuck - oo cry.

3. Cuck - oo! Cuck - oo! Wake up! Be spry!

Regina Caeli

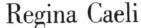

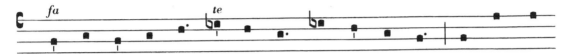

Re - gí - na caé - li lae - tá - re, al - le - lú - ia: Qui - a quem
(O Queen of Heaven rejoice, alleluia:) *(Because He Whom*

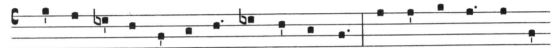

me - ru - ís - ti por - tá - re, al - le - lú - ia: Re - sur - ré - xit, si - cut
thou wast found worthy to bear, alleluia:) *(Has risen as He*

dí - xit, al - le - lú - ia: O - ra pro nó - bis Dé - um, al - le - lú - ia.
said, alleluia:) *(Pray for us to God, alleluia.)*

How often do you sing *te* instead of *ti* in this chant?

O Filii et Filiae

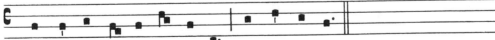

Al - le - lú - ia, al - le - lú - ia, al - le - lú - ia. *Repeat Alleluias after each stanza.*
Al - le - lu - ia, al - le - lu - ia, al - le - lu - ia.

1. O fí - li - i et fí - li - ae, Rex cae - lé - stis, Rex gló - ri - ae,
1. Ye sons and daugh-ters of the Lord, The King of glo - ry, King a-dored,

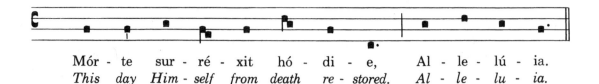

Mór - te sur - ré - xit hó - di - e, Al - le - lú - ia.
This day Him - self from death re - stored. Al - le - lu - ia.

2. Et mane príma sábbati,
   Ad óstium monuménti
   Accessérunt discípuli, allelúia.

2. *On Sunday morn at break of day,*
   The faithful women went their way,
   To seek the tomb where Jesus lay.
   Alleluia.

3. In álbis sédens Angelus
   Praedíxit muliéribus:
   In Galiláea est Dóminus, allelúia.

3. *The angel clad in white they see,*
   "The Lord ye seek is risen," said he,
   "And goes before to Galilee."
   Alleluia.

Easter Bells

S. C.

WILL EARHART

mi so fa re

1. East-er bells are chim-ing, chim-ing clear. _____
2. Glad the mes-sage ring-ing o - ver - head. _____

do so la ti

1. East-er bells are chim-ing, chim-ing,
2. Glad the mes-sage ring-ing o - ver -

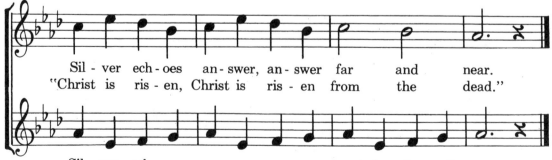

Sil - ver ech-oes an-swer, an-swer far and near.
"Christ is ris-en, Christ is ris-en from the dead."

Sil - ver ech-oes an-swer, an-swer sweet-ly far and near.
head. "The Lord is ris-en, He is ris-en from the dead."

The Blossoms Are White

SHEILA GALVIN

IRISH FOLK TUNE

la   ti   do

1. Oh, the blos-soms are white as the new-fall-en snow,
2. Oh, the bird in the tree and the wind from the sea

And a sing-ing wind is blow-ing from the sea;
Make a mel-o-dy as bright as dawn of day;

And we're hear-ing the song as we're stroll-ing a-long
And the song that they sing is the song of the spring

That the black-bird sings on ev-'ry bush and tree.
And of snow-y blos-soms white a-long the way.

Creation

MARY DALY

SISTER JOHN JOSEPH, C.S.J.

so

God made the sun to shine, the winds to blow,

re   fi   so

He made the rain to fall and grass to grow.

God made the sky, the moon, and stars, He made the birds, and trees, and flow'rs.

God made all things and found them___ good.

Name the key of this song. What does the cut time tell you?

When Spring Is Here

BETH M. JAEGER

CORNELIUS GURLITT
Adapted

Not too fast

1. I al - ways feel like sing - ing when I know that spring is here,
2. And when the gen - tle rain - drops fall, they al - ways seem to sing,

For then the mer - ry black-birds chat - ter in the wil - lows near.
The cool - ing show-ers ev - er help the flow - ers bloom in___ spring.

I al - ways feel like sing - ing and it fills my heart with joy
And when I see the but - ter-cups and lu - pine, oh, so blue,

To know there's so much beau - ty for ev - 'ry girl and boy.
I know God loves His chil - dren and all the beau - ty too.

62

Old Folks at Home

STEPHEN COLLINS FOSTER

mi

Way down up-on the Swa-nee Riv-er, Far, far a - way,
All up and down the whole cre - a - tion Sad - ly I roam,
do. . . . . do . . . fa . . . do . . . . . . so

There's where my heart is turn-ing ev-er, There's where the old folks___ stay.
Still long-ing for the old plan-ta-tion, And for the old folks at home.
do . . . . do . . . fa . . . do . . . . . so . . . . . do

CHORUS

All the world is sad and drear-y Ev - 'ry-where I roam;
so . . . so . . . . do . . do . . . . fa . . . fa . . . . do

Oh, ev - er does my heart grow wea - ry, Far from the old folks at home.
do . . . . do . . . fa . . do . . . . so . . . . do

63

Pentecost

The Holy Spirit will teach you whatsoever I shall have said to you.

Veni Creator Spiritus

1. Vé - ni Cre - á - tor Spí - ri - tus, Mén - tes tu - ó - rum ví - si - ta:
(Come, Creator Spirit,)   *(Visit the souls of Thy faithful,)*

Im - ple su - pér - na grá - ti - a Quae tu cre - á - sti pé - cto - ra.
(Fill with heavenly grace)   *(The hearts which Thou didst create.)*

2. Dé - o Pá - tri sit gló - ri - a, Et Fí - li - o, qui a mór - tu - is
(Glory be to God the Father,)   *(and to the Son who rose from*

Sur - ré - xit, ac Pa - rá - cli - to, In sae - cu - ló - rum sáe - cu - la. A - men.
the dead,) *(and to the Paraclete,)*   *(World without end.)*

64

Prayer to the Holy Spirit

Adapted by SISTER JOHN JOSEPH, C.S.J.

SISTER MARY ANTONE, C.S.J.

O grant us Thy grac-es, great Spir-it of Wis-dom. En-light-en our minds with Thy bless-ings And kin-dle the hearts of Thy faith-ful With love for Thy glo-ry and hon-or.

O Holy Spirit

TRADITIONAL

JOSEPH DALY

O Ho-ly Spir-it, O God of Love, Send down Thy grac-es from Heav'n a-bove. En-light-en my mind, In-flame my heart, that in Thy glo-ry I may have part.

65

Ring, Ring the Banjo!

STEPHEN C. FOSTER

1. The time is nev-er drear-y If a fel-low nev-er groans;
2. Oh! nev-er count the bub-bles While there's wa-ter in the spring.

The la-dies nev-er wea-ry With the rat-tle of the bones.
A fel-low has no trou-bles While he's got this song to sing.

Then come a-gain, Su-san-na, By the gas-light of the moon;
The beau-ties of cre-a-tion Will ___ nev-er lose their charm

We'll turn the old pi-an-o When the ban-jo's out of tune.
While I roam the old plan-ta-tion With my true love on my arm.

CHORUS

Ring, ring the ban-jo! I like that good old song.

Come a-gain my true love; Oh, where you been so long?

Sacerdos et Pontifex

Sa - cér - dos et Pón - ti - fex   et vir - tú - tum ó - pi - fex, pá - stor
(Priest and pontiff,   *strong in mighty deeds,)*   *(Good*

bó - ne in pó - pu - lo,   sic pla - cu - í - sti Dó - mi - no. *T.P.* Al - le - lú - ia.
shepherd of thy people,   *thou hast pleased the Lord.)*

Confirma hoc

do-ti-do

Con - fír - ma hoc Dé - us   quod o - pe - rá - tus es in nó - bis,   a tém - plo sán -
(Confirm, O God, what Thou hast accomplished among us,)   *(from Thy*

cto tú - o,   quod est in Je - rú - sa - lem. ℣ Gló - ri - a Pá - tri, et Fí -
holy temple which is in Jerusalem.)

li - o,   et Spi - rí - tu - i Sán - cto. ℟ Síc - ut é - rat in prin - cí - pi - o,

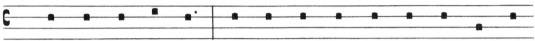

et nunc, et sém - per, et in sáe - cu - la sae - cu - ló - rum.

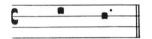

Repeat antiphon Confirma hoc *to first double bar.*

A - men.

This neum ( ) is a *porrectus*. It is made up of three notes like this ( ).
In a *porrectus* the second note is always the lowest of the three.
In this *porrectus* the syllables are *do-ti-do.*

Song of Praise

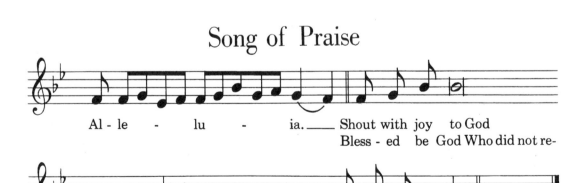

Al - le - lu - ia. ___ Shout with joy   to God
            Bless - ed   be God Who did not re-

all   the earth,   sing ye a psalm to   praise His Ho - ly Name.
ject   my pray'r,   and did not withdraw His mer - cy from   me. *Repeat Alleluia.*

O Trinity of Blessed Light

1. O Tri - ni - ty of bless-ed light, O U - ni - ty of — prince-ly might,
2. To Thee our morn-ing song of praise, To Thee our eve - ning pray'r we raise,

The fie - ry sun now goes his way; Shed Thou with-in our hearts Thy ray.
Thy glo - ry sup - pliant we a - dore, For - ev - er and for - ev - er - more.

To the Trinity

PAUL STAUDER, S.J.

ALICE TORNOVISH

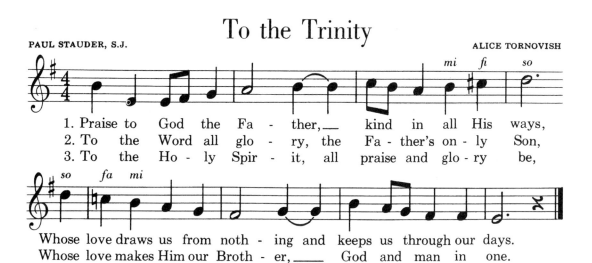

1. Praise to God the Fa - ther, — kind in all His ways,
2. To the Word all glo - ry, the Fa - ther's on - ly Son,
3. To the Ho - ly Spir - it, all praise and glo - ry be,

Whose love draws us from noth - ing and keeps us through our days.
Whose love makes Him our Broth - er, — God and man in one.
Whose pres - ence makes us shar - ers in His Di - vin - i - ty.

A woman clothed with the sun, and the moon under her feet,
and on her head a crown of twelve stars.

Mother All Merciful

NORWEGIAN ROUND

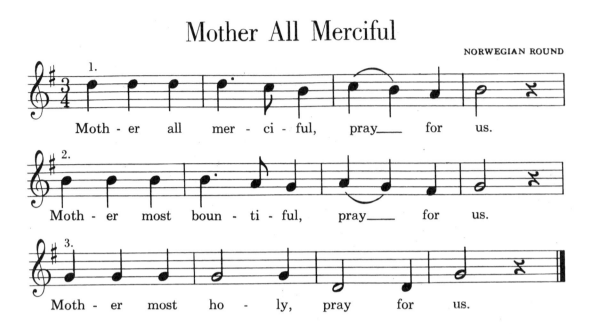

Moth - er all mer - ci - ful, pray___ for us.

Moth - er most boun - ti - ful, pray___ for us.

Moth - er most ho - ly, pray for us.

Virgin Wholly Marvelous

FOURTH CENTURY   TRADITIONAL

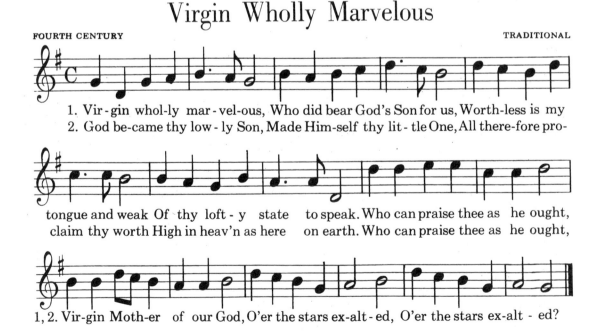

1. Vir-gin whol-ly mar-vel-ous, Who did bear God's Son for us, Worth-less is my
2. God be-came thy low-ly Son, Made Him-self thy lit-tle One, All there-fore pro-

tongue and weak Of thy loft-y state to speak. Who can praise thee as he ought,
claim thy worth High in heav'n as here on earth. Who can praise thee as he ought,

1, 2. Vir-gin Moth-er of our God, O'er the stars ex-alt-ed, O'er the stars ex-alt-ed?

70

America, the Beautiful

KATHARINE LEE BATES

SAMUEL A. WARD

1. O beau-ti-ful for spa-cious skies, For am-ber waves of grain,
2. O beau-ti-ful for pa-triot dream That sees be-yond the years

For pur-ple moun-tain maj-es-ties A-bove the fruit-ed plain!
Thine al-a-bas-ter cit-ies gleam, Un-dimmed by hu-man tears!

1,2. A-mer-i-ca! A-mer-i-ca! God shed His grace on thee,

And crown thy good with broth-er-hood From sea to shin-ing sea!

Flag Song

LYDIA AVERY COONLEY WARD

BETTY LUNT

With spirit

1. Out on the breeze, o'er land and seas, A beau-ti-ful ban-ner is
2. O-ver the brave long may it wave,___ Peace to the world ev-er

stream-ing, Shin-ing its stars, splen-did its bars, Un-der the sun-shine 'tis
bring-ing, While to the stars linked with the bars Hearts will for-ev-er be

gleam-ing. Hail to the flag, the dear, bon-ny flag, The
sing-ing. Hail to the flag, the dear, bon-ny flag, The

flag that is red, white and blue.

flag that is red, white and blue.

Grant, we beseech Thee, O mighty and merciful God, that the Holy Spirit coming to us may make us the temple of His glory by dwelling in us.

Christist, the Glory of the Sky

FIFTH CENTURY
Translated by R. CAMPBELL

17th CENTURY HYMN

1. Christ, the glo-ry of the sky, Christ, of earth the hope se-cure;
2. Praise the Fa-ther, praise the Son, Spir-it blest, to thee be praise;

On-ly Son of God most high, Off-spring of a Maid-en pure.
To th'e-ter-nal Three in One Glo-ry be through end-less days.

In four measures of this song you can find the complete descending major scale.
Put the measures together on the chalkboard.

Cor Jesu Sacratissimum

Cor Jé-su sa-cra-tís-si-mum, mi-se-ré-re no-bis.
(Heart of Jesus in the Blessed Sacrament, have mercy on us.)

Our May Queen

S. R. M.

BOHEMIAN FOLK TUNE

1. Where blue vio-lets may be seen, Where the grass grows soft and green,
2. We placed flow-ers at her feet, We hung gar-lands fresh and sweet,

There we crowned Our La-dy fair: Charm-ing queen of May-time.
Then we sang our hymns of joy, Through the hap-py May-time.

What is the key of this song?

The Story of Père Marquette

The Players

NARRATOR	RED MOOSE
ARMAND	GREAT BOW
JEAN	GRAY WOLF
PÈRE MARQUETTE	BEAR CLAW
JACQUES	JOLIET
INDIANS—*Braves, Squaws, Children, etc.*	

NARRATOR. It was evening on the St. Lawrence River. Close to the northern shore, not far from the city of Quebec, a bark canoe came swiftly upstream. Strong arms dipped the paddles and hearty voices sang a lively song. There were four men in the canoe: three French voyageurs and a Jesuit priest, Père Marquette, who had come to New France to preach the gospel to the Indians.

Up the River

S. C.

FRENCH-CANADIAN

Up the riv-er now we go to the cit-y of Que-bec, And we sing as we trav-el a-long.____ All the birds that fly a-bove and the fish that swim be-low, Oh, they all want to join our song.____

ARMAND. My friends, do not sing so loudly. On the south bank of the river I see a band of Iroquois.

JEAN. Iroquois! Paddle faster, men! I do not wish to roast for an Iroquois dinner!

PÈRE MARQUETTE. But surely the Iroquois are not cannibals!

JACQUES. Ah, but they are, mon Père! They believe that if they eat the heart of a brave man they will be filled with his courage. I prefer that they eat something else!

PÈRE MARQUETTE. Listen! They are singing, and the drums are beating. Is it a war song?

Deer Hunting Song

IROQUOIS

Boys: Ar - row be sure, find the war - y deer!
Chorus: Ar - row be sure, find the war - y deer!
Boys: Deep in the for - est dark, they are hid - ing there.
Chorus: Deep in the for - est dark, they are hid - ing there.

Play on the tom-tom a rhythm like this:
Play the accented notes loudly.

ARMAND. (*When the song is finished*) No, mon Père, that was not a war song. It is merely a hunting song. The Iroquois sing to their arrows and tell them to find the deer.

PÈRE MARQUETTE. Perhaps they have not seen us.

JACQUES. The Iroquois see everything. They have seen us. But we are safe on this side of the river. It is so wide their arrows cannot reach us.

JEAN. And ahead are the walls of Quebec. We shall escape this time.

NARRATOR. And so Père Marquette came to Quebec. Often he thought of the savage Iroquois and wished he might be sent to preach to them. But instead he was ordered to travel still farther westward to the shores of Lake Superior. There he preached to the Algonquians, baptized them, and offered Holy Mass for them. He loved his Indians very much and they loved the Blackrobe who had come to teach them. Sometimes they told him of other tribes who had never heard of the Gospel.

RED MOOSE. There are many tribes, Blackrobe—more than the leaves on the trees.

PÈRE MARQUETTE. And none of them know of their Heavenly Father or of Christ His Son, Who died to save all men?

GREAT BOW. They worship the spirits in the water and the forests.

PÈRE MARQUETTE. There are no spirits in the water or the forest. The Great Spirit Who dwells above, whom you call Gitchie Manitou and we call Heavenly Father, has filled the rivers with fish and the forests with birds and animals, so that His children will have food to eat.

GREAT BOW. Far away there is a great river that is called the Father of Waters. The tribes say that the spirits can swallow a canoe.

PÈRE MARQUETTE. Do not listen to such foolish talk, Great Bow. You are a man. You do not believe the stories of children.

NARRATOR. Often Great Bow would sing for Père Marquette, and Red Moose would play on his flute. Sometimes they sang the song of the sunrise.

Deep in the Forest

ETHEL CROWNINSHIELD

OJIBWAY

1. Deep in the for - est, dark is the night, But low in the sky I see a bright light. Run, lit - tle shad - ows, swift - ly a - way! The bright morn-ing star is call - ing the day.

2. High on the hill and low on the plain, The warm gold-en sun will soon come a - gain. Shad-ows, run quick - ly, run while you may! The bright morn-ing star has called to the day.

NARRATOR. One day a band of Illinois Indians came to the mission. They asked permission to see the Blackrobe.

RED MOOSE. Blackrobe, this chief is from the country of the Illinois. His name is Gray Wolf. He wishes to speak with you.

PÈRE MARQUETTE. Let the chief speak!

GRAY WOLF. Blackrobe, will you come to the country of my people who live on the banks of the Father of Waters? My people wish to learn about the Gitchie Manitou.

PÈRE MARQUETTE. I will come, but first I must learn the language of the Illinois.

GRAY WOLF. That is good. My people do not know of the Great Spirit. They are like leaves that drift on the water of the Great River. They do not know where the days go, nor where men go, nor what the end will be.

Down the Stream

DERRICK NORMAN LEHMER COLLECTION

MIWOK

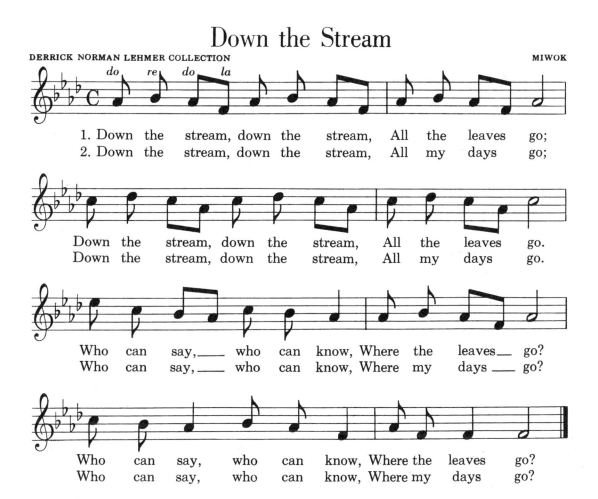

1. Down the stream, down the stream, All the leaves go;
2. Down the stream, down the stream, All my days go;

Down the stream, down the stream, All the leaves go.
Down the stream, down the stream, All my days go.

Who can say,___ who can know, Where the leaves__ go?
Who can say,___ who can know, Where my days ___ go?

Who can say, who can know, Where the leaves go?
Who can say, who can know, Where my days go?

NARRATOR. One night, unfriendly Indians attacked the little village. The Catholic Indians had to hide in the forest. Great Bow and Red Moose took Père Marquette in their canoe and paddled away quickly. They could hear the drums beating behind them and the wild music of the war song.

War Song

BLACKFOOT

Hee - yah hee - yah hah-yah hah-yah, Hee-yah hee - yah hah-yah hah-yah,

Hee - yah hee - yah hah-yah hah - yah, Hah - yah-hay, hah - yah-hay!

Hah - yah hah - yah hah - yah - yah - yah - hay!

Play a steady tom-tom beat like this

NARRATOR. Père Marquette wanted to learn more about the Great River, but Gray Wolf could only tell him that it was called the Mississippi, the Father of Waters, and that it flowed far toward the south. Then Gray Wolf went back to his people and Père Marquette began to study the language of the Illinois with his friend, Red Moose, who knew the language. He thought often of the great Mississippi. He hoped that someday he would find the Great River. He liked to hear the Indian mothers singing lullabies to their little children.

Go to Sleep

MENOMINEE

Go to sleep,— my lit-tle one. All the lit-tle rab-bits sleep.— All the ea-gles in their nests.— And all the fox-es in their dens.— The owl has cried in the for-est deep. Go to sleep, my lit-tle ba-by.—

GREAT BOW. Blackrobe, we shall take you to the white man's village.
There you will be safe.

PÈRE MARQUETTE. But someday I shall return to my mission, if it is
God's will.

RED MOOSE. Great Bow, we must sing to the Blackrobe. We must
make him glad again. Let us sing the dancing song while
we paddle.

Dance Song

CHIPPEWA

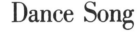

Ho, broth-ers, lis-ten   to the drums, to the drums! Loud-ly they are
Now the drums are

beat-ing for the dance, for the dance. Come, ev-'ry brave and maid-en, come and
beat-ing for the dance, for the dance. Come, ev-'ry brave and maid-en, come and

join the danc-ing. War-riors come and join the danc-ing, hah - yah - hah!
join the danc-ing. War-riors come and join the danc-ing, hah - yah - hah!

Accompany with steady beat on Indian drum.

82

NARRATOR. And so Père Marquette came to the village of Sault Sainte Marie. There he met a brave Frenchman, Louis Joliet, who had heard of the Great River. Together they planned to explore it. One day they set out with their Indian friends on the long journey. They sang as they paddled their canoe. Sometimes they sang the songs of the French.

Port of St. Marie

FRENCH-CANADIAN

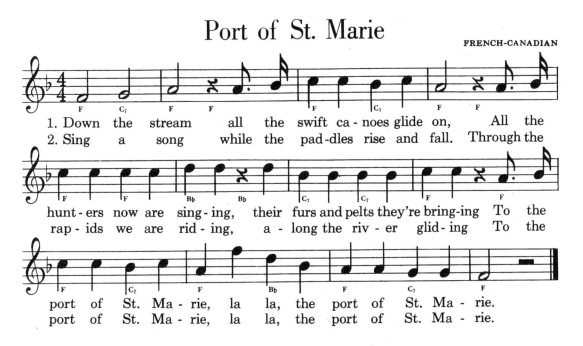

1. Down the stream all the swift ca-noes glide on, All the
2. Sing a song while the pad-dles rise and fall. Through the

hunt-ers now are sing-ing, their furs and pelts they're bring-ing To the
rap-ids we are rid-ing, a-long the riv-er glid-ing To the

port of St. Ma-rie, la la, the port of St. Ma-rie.
port of St. Ma-rie, la la, the port of St. Ma-rie.

NARRATOR. The days went by as they paddled along the waterways. When the moon was full and the nights were filled with its silver light, they would travel all night. Then the Indians would sing the song of the birch canoe.

My Bark Canoe

CHIPPEWA-OJIBWAY

In the moon-light, the long hours through I glide — My —

bark ca-noe, my bark ca-noe, my bark ca-noe.

NARRATOR. At last the explorers came to the end of the waterways. Then they carried their canoes overland to the Wisconsin River. They hoped it would lead them to the Mississippi. As they paddled along the Wisconsin they saw buffalo grazing everywhere. Soon they came to an Indian village. A tall chief stood on the bank to welcome them.

BEAR CLAW. I am Bear Claw. I am chief of this village. The Blackrobe and his friends are welcome to our village. We have heard of the Gitchie Manitou. The Blackrobe must tell us more about Him.

PÈRE MARQUETTE. We are honored to visit the village of Bear Claw.

BEAR CLAW. We shall hunt the buffalo. When the hunters return we shall feast and then we shall hear the story of the Gitchie Manitou.

Buffalo Dance

OJIBWAY

War - riors come and join me, we shall hunt the buf - fa - lo

Graz - ing on the prai - rie, man - y, man - y buf - fa - lo.

Graz-ing on the prai-rie, man-y, man-y buf-fa-lo. We shall kill buf-fa-lo.

Play this rhythm on the tom-tom.

NARRATOR. After the hunt and the feast the Indians held a council. Many chiefs and braves came to listen as Père Marquette told them of the Gitchie Manitou, the Great Spirit Who made the world. He told them of the Child Who was born in Bethlehem, Who was the Son of God, Who died on the cross to save all men.

NARRATOR. Then the Indians told Père Marquette and Joliet how they could find the Great River. When the council ended the explorers paddled on down the Wisconsin. At last their canoes entered the broad stream of the Mississippi.

PÈRE MARQUETTE. May God be praised! We have found the Mississippi! May He bless this river which I name for His blessed Mother, the River of the Immaculate Conception.

JOLIET. Our Lady has led us to her mighty river. Let us ask her to protect us as we travel upon it. Let us sing a hymn in her honor.

Ave Maris Stella

TRADITIONAL

A - ve má - ris stél - la, Ma - rí - a!
Hail, bright star of o - cean, Ma - ri - a!

Dé - i Má - ter ál - ma, Ma - rí - a!
God's own Moth - er ho - ly, Ma - ri - a!

At - que sém - per Vír - go,— Fé - lix cáe - li pór - ta,
Ev - er sin - less Vir - gin,— Heav - en's bless - ed por - tal,

Ma - rí - a, Ma - rí - a!
Ma - ri - a, Ma - ri - a!

NARRATOR. For days and days the explorers paddled down the Mississippi. They came to the country of the Illinois. Père Marquette told the Illinois the story of the Gitchie Manitou and Christ, His Son, Who died to save all men. After many days with the Illinois, the travellers paddled down the river.

PÈRE MARQUETTE. We have come many miles; and still the Great River flows to the south.

RED MOOSE. Far to the south there is a great sea into which the river flows. That is what the old warriors say.

JOLIET. We shall try to find the great sea.

NARRATOR. They paddled on and on. They passed a great brown river which the Indians called the Missouri, the muddy river. Days later they came to the mouth of another great river, clear and green. This, said the Indians who lived there, was the Ohio, the beautiful river.

All along Père Marquette preached to the Indians. They welcomed him and were glad to listen. One night as they made their camp, they heard drums beating, and shouts and singing in the distance.

PÈRE MARQUETTE. What are they singing, Red Moose? Is it a war song?

RED MOOSE. No, it is the game of the moccasin. Listen.

Game Song

OMAHA

Now I shall hide the peb-ble, hide the peb-ble, hide the peb-ble,

Now I shall hide the peb-ble un-der-neath a moc-ca-sin.

Take a stick and beat the ground and see if you can

strike the peb-ble Un-der-neath the moc-ca-sin.

Play this rhythm on the tom-tom.

86

RED MOOSE. Blackrobe, we have come to the country of tribes we do not know. It is time to turn back. They may be unfriendly.

PÈRE MARQUETTE. You are right, Red Moose. We gain nothing by going on. We may lose our lives.

JOLIET. We have found the Mississippi. We claim all the land its waters drain for the King of France. We have explored many miles. To-morrow we shall paddle upstream again.

NARRATOR. So, in the morning, they turned the prows of their canoes toward the north. As they went upstream, dipping their paddles in the swift current, they sang the songs of Frenchmen and the songs of Indians. Often they sang to Our Lady and asked her protection. And Our Lady heard them, and spread her mantle over them, and brought them safely home.

Ave Maris Stella

TRADITIONAL

A - ve má - ris stél - la, Ma - rí - a!
Hail, bright star of o - cean, Ma - ri - a!

Dé - i Má - ter ál - ma, Ma - rí - a!
God's own Moth - er ho - ly, Ma - ri - a!

At - que sém - per Vír - go, Fé - lix cáe - li
Ev - er sin - less Vir - gin, Heav - en's bless - ed

pór - ta, Ma - rí - a, Ma - rí - a!
por - tal, Ma - ri - a, Ma - ri - a!

We Sing the Mass

Sometimes we see the chant conducted with movements of the hand. This is called *chironomy*.

The up-movement, which helps to give life or energy to chant, is called an *arsis* (⌒····). The down-movement, which gives a feeling of quiet or repose, is called a *thesis* (⌒ ⌒).

You will sing the chant better if you watch these hand movements carefully. In another grade you will learn to do them.

Kyrie

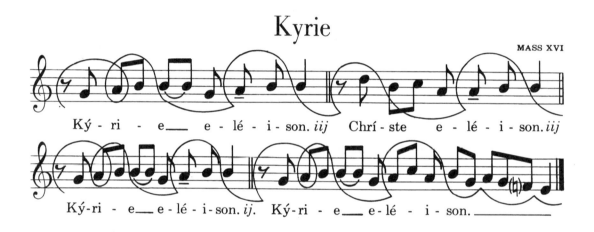

Ký - ri - e ___ e - lé - i - son. *iij* Chrí - ste e - lé - i - son. *iij*

Ký-ri - e e ___ e - lé - i - son. *ij.* Ký - ri - e e ___ e - lé - i - son. ___

Gloria

Glo - ri - a ___ in ex - cél - sis Dé - o. Et in tér - ra pax ho - mí - ni - bus

bó - nae vo - lun - tá - tis. Lau - dá - mus te. Be - ne - dí - ci - mus te.

A - do - rá - mus te. Glo - ri - fi - cá - mus te.

88

Grá - ti - as á - gi-mus ti - bi pro-pter má-gnam gló - ri - am tú - am.

Dó - mi - ne Dé-us, Rex cae-lé - stis, Dé-us Pá - ter o - mní-po-tens.

Dó - mi - ne Fí - li u - ni - gé - ni - te, Jé - su Chrí - ste.

Dó - mi - ne Dé - us, A-gnus Dé - i, Fí - li - us Pá - tris.

Qui tól - lis pec - cá - ta mún - di, mi - se - ré - re nó - bis.

Qui tól - lis pec-cá - ta mún-di, su - sci - pe de-pre-ca - ti - ó-nem nó-stram.

Qui sé - des ad déx - te - ram Pá - tris, mi - se - ré - re nó - bis.

Quó - ni - am tu só - lus sán-ctus. Tu só - lus Dó - mi - nus.

89

Tu só-lus Al-tís-si-mus, Jé-su Chrí - ste. Cum Sán-cto Spí-ri - tu,

in gló-ri-a Dé-i Pá - tris. A - men.

Credo 1

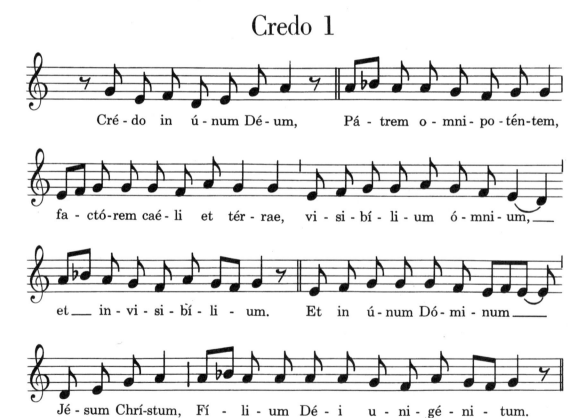

Cré-do in ú-num Dé-um, Pá - trem o-mni-po-tén-tem,

fa-ctó-rem caé-li et tér-rae, vi-si-bí-li-um ó-mni-um,

et in-vi-si-bí-li-um. Et in ú-num Dó-mi-num

Jé-sum Chrí-stum, Fí - li-um Dé-i u-ni-gé-ni-tum.

Et ex Pá-tre ná-tum an-te ó-mni-a saé-cu-la. Dé-

90

um de Dé - o, lú - men de lú - mi - ne,_____ Dé-um vé-rum de

Dé - o vé - ro. Gé - ni-tum, non fá-ctum, con-sub-stan-ti - á - lem

Pá - tri: per quem ó - mni - a fá - cta sunt. Qui pro-pter nos

hó - mi - nes, et pro-pter nó-stram sa - lú - tem de-scén-dit de caé - lis.

Et in-car-ná-tus est de Spí - ri - tu Sán-cto ex___ Ma - rí -

a Vír - gi - ne: Et___ hó-mo fá - ctus est. Cru - ci - fí - xus ét -

i - am pro nó - bis: sub___Pón-ti - o Pi - lá - to pás - sus, et

se - púl - tus est. Et re-sur-ré - xit tér - ti - a dí - e, se -

cún-dum Scrip-tú - ras.　Et　a - scén - dit in caé - lum: sé - det

ad déx - te - ram Pá - tris.　Et＿ í - te - rum ven - tú - rus est cum gló - ri -

a,＿＿＿ ju - di - cá - re　vi - vos et mór - tu - os: cú - jus ré - gni

non é - rit fí - nis.　Et　in Spí - ri - tum Sán-ctum Dó - mi - num,＿

et＿ vi - vi - fi - cán-tem:　qui ex Pá - tre Fi - li - ó - que pro -

cé - dit.　Qui cum Pá - tre et Fí - li - o　si - mul ad - o - rá - tur,

et＿con-glo - ri - fi - cá - tur: qui lo - cú - tus est per Pro-phé - tas.

Et＿ú - nam sán-ctam ca - thó - li - cam＿　et＿ a - po - stó - li -

cam Ec - clé - si - am. Con - fí - te - or ú - num ba - ptís - ma in re - mis - si - ó - nem pec - ca - tó - rum. Et ex - spé - cto re - sur - re - cti - ó - nem mor - tu - ó - rum. Et __ ví - tam ven - tú - ri saé - cu - li. A - men. __

Preface

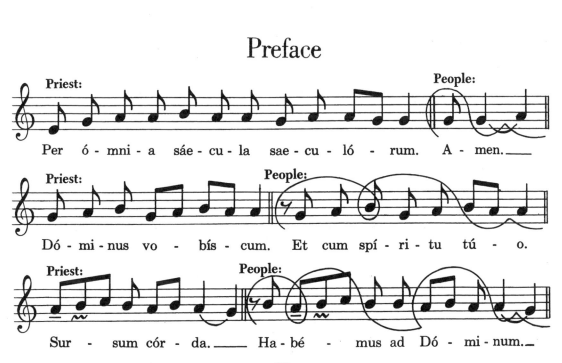

Priest: Per ó - mni - a sáe - cu - la sae - cu - ló - rum. **People:** A - men. __

Priest: Dó - mi - nus vo - bís - cum. **People:** Et cum spí - ri - tu tú - o.

Priest: Sur - sum cór - da. __ **People:** Ha - bé - mus ad Dó - mi - num. __

Priest:

Grá - ti - as ___ a - gá - mus Dó - mi - no ___ Dé - o nó - stro.

People:

Di - gnum et jús - tum est. ___

Sanctus

MASS XVI

Sán - ctus, ___ Sán - ctus ___ Sán - ctus Dó - mi - nus

Dé - us Sá - ba - oth. Plé - ni sunt caé - li et tér - ra

gló - ri - a tú - a. Ho - sán - na ___ in ex - cél - sis. ___

Benedictus

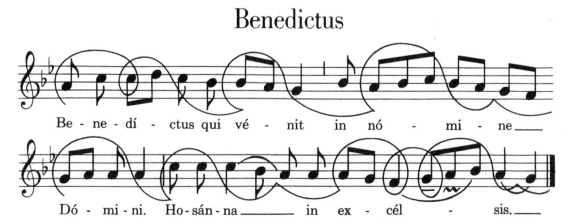

Be - ne - dí - ctus qui vé - nit in nó - mi - ne ___

Dó - mi - ni. Ho - sán - na ___ in ex - cél - sis. ___

Agnus Dei

A - gnus Dé - i, _____ qui tól - lis __ pec - cá - ta __

mún - di: mi - se - ré - re __ nó - bis.

A - gnus Dé - i, qui tól - lis pec - cá - ta mún - di:

mi - se - ré - re _____ nó - bis. A - gnus

Dé - i, _____ qui tól - lis __ pec - cá - ta __ mún - di:

dó - na no - bis __ pá - cem.

Before the Blessing

Priest: Ite Missa est.
Choir:

De - o _____ grá ti - as.

This is one of several ways in which *Deo Gratias* may be sung.

95